Advance

A Little Touch of Cancer and How It Made Me Well

"Wonderfully conversational, informative, heartfelt, and inspiring!"
—STACEY LOGAN, Broadway actress, *Beauty and the Beast,*
Candide, High Society, Crazy for You

"An interesting story, written by an obviously very accomplished and cosmopolitan woman. She triumphed over a formidable obstacle with admirable intellectual and physical fortitude."
—BURTON J. LEE III, MD, Senior Attending, Lymphoma Service,
and Clinical Professor of Medicine, Memorial Sloan Kettering Cancer
Center, 1988. Physician to President G. H. W. Bush, 1989–1993

"This is a love story—about the discovery of new love with an old partner and love for self through forgiveness and understanding. It is about second chances catalyzed by a terrifying diagnosis. I loved it!"
—PATRICIA F. SULLIVAN, NRDC Consultant

"This beautifully written memoir tells us the most intimate of stories, but makes it universal as well as deeply personal. Informative in terms of the ins and outs of her treatment, the author gives an incredible portrait of what it is to live through cancer."
—MEREDITH TUCKER, Casting Director, *Boardwalk Empire*

A Little Touch of Cancer
and How It Made Me Well

A Little Touch of Cancer
and How It Made Me Well

One Woman's Travels
through Ovarian Cancer

Betsy Horn

SERENITY PUBLICATIONS

ISBN: 978-061589-8773
Library of Congress Control Number: to come
Printed in the United States of America

Cover photograph: Margaret Gibbons, NY

Back cover photograph: Richard Jordan, NY

Book Cover: julieteninbaum.com

Book design by Victoria Hartman

This book may be ordered from www.amazon.com
and other retailers.

This book may also be ordered at www.betsyhorn.com

For John, who has been my rock,

and for

Alexander, Iona and Miranda,

whose existence gives me infinite joy

Acknowledgments

While I have no interest in writing an academy awards acceptance speech, there are a number of people to thank for a long, seemingly endless journey to make this book ready.

First, there are four editors to whom I sing songs of praise. Jemma Lough began the process and received a first draft which was really a 'mess of pottage.' Next came the inestimable Walter Bode, to whom, if I write at all well, I owe gratitude and thanks for his infinite wisdom and patience. Ditto for my soul sister, Suzanne Fox, who has helped me finish and calibrate with a watchful eye. Last but not least, my daughter, Anastasia Edwards, author and editor, tailored my outline in the early stages, turned my thoughts into useable topics, and always knew how to deal tactfully with doubt or discouragement.

Thanks go to Miles Dumont, Peggotty Gilson, Barbara Hackett, Barbara Sloan, Dr. Florence Licata and others I may have forgotten for taking the time to read what I sent them and to comment truthfully. I appreciated it then, and still do. Thanks as well to John Horn, who, like Miss Adelaide from *Guys and Dolls*, had to keep doing the same thing over and over—in this case, reading and re-reading what appeared to be the same material; unlike poor Adelaide, he never developed that "bad, bad cold." Special thanks to my dear friend, Mary Louise Hamill, and to my brother, Llewellyn Ross, for their courage in commenting on an important section, which needed alterations and where I was wavering. Thanks to Abby Stokes; this book rests on the back of the computing skills she teaches, and for many years she has guided me through the shoals of Internet conventions and publishing wisdom, offering priceless tidbits all sprinkled with humor. Thanks to my daughter, Philippa Cully, who, in spite of her busy life, came to Connecticut to help me pack intelligently for the first trip to Switzerland and gave suggestions about self-publishing way before that possibility was on my own horizon.

I am deeply grateful to all of the friends who were so wonderfully kind and caring during my illness, and from whom I learned so much. Very special thanks in that regard go to Susan and William Kinsolving, Rick Jordan, Scott Belter and Dale McBrearity. I will never forget that Susan kept a small packed valise at the bottom of her staircase in case I needed her day or night. Rick's upbeat arrivals kept me sane as did Scott when I was alone at the farm. Dale is an angel here on earth. Thanks to Gloria Correa who kept me eating the right food and bolstered my spirits whenever they were sagging, and to Christopher Marlowe, my friend, accompanist and arranger for years, and Scott Barnes for their compassion and care.

Thanks, too, to Isabel and Winston Fowlkes, Brooke Duchin, Peter Duchin, Hiram Williams and Peter Vaughn, Alec and Drika Purvis, Rita and Marvin Ginsky, Patricia Sullivan, Phyllis and Tony Potter, Virginia and Tony Montgomery, Victoria Shaw, Acklin and John Dunning, Nonie Wyckoff, Robert Pincus-Witton and Leon Hecht, the late Margaret Gardner, Annette Nicolls, Mary Rendall, Richey Smith, Sally Fleming and Barbara Christian of the Marion Foundation. If I have forgotten to name any others, it is not for lack of appreciation.

To my doctors and therapists, I give heartfelt thanks not only for the care and concern they showed, but for the work we have done and continue to do together: Dr. Peter Schwartz of Yale-New Haven

Hospital; Dr. John Postley of New York Physicians; Dr. Thomas Rau, Mr. Wolfgang Haas, and Mr. Michael Falkner, all of the Paracelsus Clinic in Switzerland; Dr. Ara Elmajian of Vancouver; Dr. Stephen Bowne of New York; Dr. Jack Light of Lake Worth, Florida; Dr. Nancy Lasak of New York; Scott Suvow; Jan Troy; Seth Morrison; Karin Stephan; Dr. Jane M. Miner; and, most recently, Dr. James Gordon, founder of the Center for Mind Body Medicine, in Washington, D.C., and my wonderful general practitioner in Florida, Guy Ulrich.

A special 'hug' goes to Betsy Baird and Helen Modell, both at Yale-New Haven Hospital and to Nadine Jean-Baptiste, John Postley's right hand in New York. The world should know that the wheels in health care are greased by people like you. Lisalotte Tolotti at the Paracelsus Clinic also has my respectful thanks; she is the only nurse who has ever penetrated without difficulty my left arm and who can successfully, painlessly insert a needle into the most difficult of veins, receiving only a wan smile for her efforts.

Three of the women who played key roles in this story died before they could read the book or my thanks to them. Gail Miller gave me warm sisterhood, encouragement, delicious blueberry pancakes and Hawaiian hospitality at her historic house in Kauai, in whose guest cottage I sat mornings, smelling the plumeria trees as I scribbled. Second, she left us unexpectedly over a year ago, but without Marianne Challis' teaching and friendship, her well of bottomless love and support, I am not sure what I'd have done. Finally, thanks to the late Marion Bedrick, who sat through my entire surgery waiting for me to wake up. I am certain the celestial chorus is overjoyed to have all of these extraordinary women as choristers. I feel the heavens are surely vibrating at a higher bandwidth.

Contents

A Little Touch of Cancer
and How It Made Me Well

1

A Diagnosis

Be kind, for everyone you meet is fighting a great
battle.

— PHILO OF ALEXANDRIA

On a sparkling spring day in May 2001, I headed out of New York
City, crossed the old Triborough Bridge, and pointed my sleek green
Audi towards New Haven and my destination, the Yale-New Haven
Hospital. I had always loved driving, especially that car. Normally, I
would have enjoyed the still-uncluttered Merritt Parkway, always
bound to revive childhood memories like playing hooky from school
to go to the Ringling Brothers Circus in New York with my parents.

This was a different kind of trip, however—symbolically enough,
a Biblical seventh. I was returning to Yale's outpatient clinic to check
on a pesky ovarian cyst that had seemingly done very little for the
seven years in which I had been monitoring it. I had been told that if
it didn't grow bigger it was a good sign, but I had still been encouraged to keep up with the annual checkups. The process hadn't worried me until now. But on this day, something felt different.

This was a second attempt at the visit; the first time around I had
forgotten to book the standard pelvic sonogram. My usual Yale doctor, Peter Schwartz, had been away on vacation, leaving his residents
in charge. At the end of the physical examination, I had been told that

everything was okay. I could forget the sonogram, the residents said, as long as I was sure to come back next year. But as I headed home, Dr. Schwartz's advice echoed in my mind. *Physical exam, PAP smear and sonogram annually!* That echo niggled at me. I'm not exactly obsessive-compulsive, but let's just say I'm detail-oriented. My gut instinct had hammered away, insisting I complete the seventh exam and have the sonogram. The essential quality in any good physician-patient relationship is confidence, and Dr. Schwartz had earned that trust over the years.

Today was the day for the makeup sonogram. This time, Dr. Schwartz would be there. His presence and physical examination always reassured me. Though I didn't feel overly fearful as I drove, my usual happy-go-lucky attitude had gone AWOL. I felt distracted and unsettled, ominous thoughts and questions running through my mind as I made my way up the Merritt. Looking back at those "what-ifs," I can see that they were a mirror reflection of parts of my life at that time.

On the surface, I was living a varied and busy life. I had friends and a social life that was more than pleasant and privileged, with dinners, trips to the opera, theatre, movies, and art galleries. But I'd had no fully realized, intimate companionship in my life since my ex-husband John and I had divorced several years before, nor was I giving of myself in fulfilling ways. Professionally, I was trying to advance my small career as a cabaret singer, continuing to vocalize with my coach and to work with my accompanist, ever hopeful of a gig just around the corner. I hadn't really admitted it, but it was becoming increasingly obvious that the idea of becoming a cabaret star so late in life was pretty unrealistic. Besides, my heart had gone out of it; the energy and motivation so necessary to continue the hard work was lacking, though whether that was the realistic assessment speaking or my as-yet undiagnosed illness, I don't know. In the midst of all of this, I had also been fixing up a post-divorce house in Bethlehem, Connecticut. Like my singing career, this was another of those grand dreams: the notion that my daughters and grandchildren would love it and that this would be a much-visited family house. I wasn't yet ready to fully accept that they had their own very busy, full lives and didn't have much extra time. My myopic vision had something to do with constantly trying to play catch-up with the impact of a long ago divorce.

During the months before that May morning, what I had been able to see was how deeply masked and buried, for years, my emotions had been. Included was a large dose of anger I habitually tried to suppress or ignore. There were still issues I wanted to sort out with my daughters, often the case with children of divorce. Equally, I knew that it would be good to take a hiatus from New York and spend some time alone, down time, to create inner space and make better sense of my past. I needed to integrate all I'd learned from years of therapy and body-mind work. I hadn't done it. I was always too busy. Something else had always come first, until today.

Arriving at the Physicians Building, I pulled the parking ticket from the machine, entered the cavernous garage, finally found a space on the top floor, parked, and threw my car keys in my equally cavernous backpack, then headed to the check-in desk in the basement. As a veteran of the diagnostic department, its procedures were familiar to me. Almost by rote, I undressed, stowing my clothes in a locker, then trotted to the waiting area, where I thumbed through a dog-eared copy of People magazine, that repository of the latest celebrity gossip. When summoned, I marched to the sonogram room, the locker key bouncing on my wrist—that bounce the only sign of joy.

The drab blue gown open in back, I lay down as instructed, feet in the supporting stirrups. That gynecological position always made me feel like an overturned cavalry beetle. This time, I was suddenly reminded of an exam I'd had in London during the time I lived there. Of all the absurd names, the doctor's name was Dr. Studd and he was, in fact, quite attractive. He had the first and only gynecological stirrups in London, so he became a destination 'gynie.' The usual English practice at the time was to lie on your side to be examined, covered with a blanket like a sick horse, so stirrups were kind of kinky. With that memory, a tiny smile emerged.

The young technician with fair but cool Nordic looks arrived, greeted me, and then deftly applied the cold gel. She handed me the vaginal probe and told me to wait for instructions as to where to move it. As I obediently paused, circled, went left and right, then repeated anti-clockwise, she was studying the screen. It was impossible to interpret what had become an intense, concentrated look on her face, but I was certain I didn't like any of it one bit. I had acted stoic and unconcerned during the previous six annual sonograms because I was acting as though I was sure that nothing would be wrong. It was a pretty good act. This time, each glance at her face chipped away at any certainty I had left.

She excused herself abruptly and left the room, saying she'd return shortly, her inscrutable mask sending shivers down my spine.

She returned with a posse: two men in white lab coats, older than she was, clearly higher on the executive ladder and clearly concerned. Nodding perfunctorily at me, they went straight for the machine, like tigers diving in for the kill. Remaining focused on the screen, they chatted in tones too low for my eager ears. I now felt threatened. I imagined myself slipping into formless anonymity, more like a cipher, both body and identity at risk.

As part of a woman's annual exam, the request for a second set of x-rays, sonogram or needle biopsy has become fairly run of the mill. Just when you think you can dress and get out of there, the nurse returns. Instead of saying, "Come back next year," with a pleasant smile she announces, "The radiologist would like to do a few more pictures," or "The diagnostician wants to perform additional tests." I had had a couple of those experiences after a mammogram. The usual line is that "it's probably nothing," and it usually *is* nothing. Technicians are just being doubly sure, cross-checking to protect both themselves and their patients. Still, those requests can drive a stake into a woman's heart, generating considerable fear—especially as we get older and both the likelihood of cancer and the number of women we know that have been diagnosed rise.

One of the doctors finally did look over at me, still lying helpless, on my back, barely covered, unable to right myself and too terrified to breathe. Peering over rimless spectacles, he politely stated that after I dressed, Dr. Schwartz needed to see me upstairs. He was admirably Delphic, but inside me the adrenaline rush had started. Busy Dr. Schwartz "needing" to see me was certainly not the news I wanted. I felt my heart tighten and my toes curl under, a lifelong habit when stressed or anxious.

Distracted and fumbling, I dressed. With mock bravery I marched out of the cubicle to enter the vast elevator, huge enough to accommodate a baby elephant. I was aware of feeling lonely in that space, as I was the only passenger and one who faced uncertainty. At the dinging green light, I alit on the second floor, found a seat, and settled in nervously to wait for this next summons, thumbing through out-of-date *Oprah* magazines this time around.

I had never noticed as many pregnant women in the streets as when I was newly pregnant myself. Then, all of a sudden, the entire world seemed to be pregnant. Now, though I'd never have given it a thought an hour earlier, I realized that everyone around me had a turban, a scarf or a bald head. The faces were pretty grim or, worse, expressionless. Others, stoic, were pale and preoccupied, all clear signs of chemotherapy at work.

After what seemed an eternity, Dr. Schwartz called me in. A tall, slender man with graying hair, he has a youthful, nimble presence. His is a face that inspires confidence from the first look, and his compassionate smile tells you he'll look after you—or at least, you hope that's what it says.

With a steady, unwavering gaze, Dr. Schwartz told me he did not like the "expression" of my ovarian cyst and would like me in surgery as soon as possible "to have a look." Gulping, I asked him what he thought was the matter, petrified of the answer. Speaking gently but firmly, he said unhesitatingly that he suspected it was ovarian cancer. Hearing his words, I crumbled on the inside, then strangely, caught myself and thought about my posture. As the "fight or flight" response hit me, I wanted very much to stand up straight and to be strong.

The notion that my survival might now be at risk collided with the beautiful day outside, the two seeming utterly at odds. How could this be? At that moment, the ordinary flow of time stopped and everything went to "pause." The pause was to be of several years' duration, a notion I couldn't begin to fathom at that moment. Without my permission, past, present and future had been introduced in an unlikely manner, like bumper cars at a fair. Dreams and all assumptions fell away in a sweeping, downward spiral.

I felt as though I had been caught out, busted. The life I'd been leading for the past few years as the somewhat gay divorcée was over. It hadn't been that gay, anyway. Now, I was to be living according to someone else's agenda, a kind of purdah. I had already known that changes would have to be made to my life; I just hadn't expected to have to conform to someone else's calendar.

Dr. Schwartz described what he would do surgically, what he would remove, what he would leave, and the options I had. If it was cancer, I didn't have many, in fact, I had none. He would remove everything. At the time there was talk, now discounted, that keeping the cervix would provide support for the other organs, so that's what we agreed to do. The conversation was thorough, but brief and I felt completely gutted. In my mind, I'd failed at something I'd always assumed should be simple not to fail at—having a healthy body. Out of the thin, antiseptic hospital air, a new career materialized in my mind: survival.

There was nothing more to do. Shaking inside, I thanked Dr. Schwartz and promised to do all the necessary chores. I hastened away to book the date for surgery in either late May or early June, whenever the doctor had the first opening. I presented my health insurance documents, confirmed my social security number, birth date, next of kin, who to call in an emergency and all the other basic information.

This practical, administrative side of illness comes as an antiseptic aftershock to diagnosis. It is all black and white and was a struggle to handle after such devastating news. Heaven alone knows how I got out the answers and held back the tears. I guess everyone remembers their birth date and social security number unless they are in dementia. I really just wanted the privacy of my car.

In exchange for my vital statistics, I was given a handful of leaflets, an appointment for blood tests and a to-do list. A quick glance told me I had my work cut out for me. There were suggestions that I find a home caregiver if I didn't have one, and also identify people who could pick up and deliver me at appointed times, both pre- and post-op. Suddenly I had another new job, this one in human resources and personnel management. When I tried to have a good cry in the ladies room, I couldn't let go. I wasn't ready. "It will come later," I told myself as I hid there, anticipating a knock on the door from some other needy woman, perhaps as desperate and upset as I.

"If I make sure the things within my control are done exactly right," I remember thinking, "I'll have a better chance than if I leave everything to others and just assume it'll turn out all right." In a way, it was a kind of magical thinking, a belief that my own mind could control the outside world. But I was right. I later realized my attitude probably affected the outcome. At that moment, with that thinking, I became both partner and participant in the treatment process, taking an active position in my own cure.

I also remember feeling terribly disappointed, even brokenhearted, a surge of guilt momentarily overwhelming me. Unsure of whether or not it was smart to drive back to the city in this fragile condition, I remembered my invitation to a social gathering that night. It was for a seated dinner party and birthday dance. Part of me wondered how I could let down my hostess, forcing her to redo the seating so late in the day. That sounds a bit ridiculous when I think about it now. But I think it helped keep the fragments of my emotions together to revert back to some familiar social code.

The day I was diagnosed with cancer I was about to be sixty, but the twelve-year-old girl in me still needed help.

2

Sailing into the Dark

Where there's life, there's hope.　　— CICERO

Shaken, I left the Physicians Building at Yale Hospital. Just finding my car in the huge, multi-level parking garage was a challenge; I couldn't even locate my keys in the voluminous backpack I carried. My conversation with Dr. Schwartz jabbed at me. *Suspected ovarian cancer.* Judging from the piercing look in his eye, he would clearly have preferred the surgery sooner. But the first available date had been in early June—ironically, just three weeks before my 60th birthday.

Wandering around the garage, finally finding the car, I was still pondering whether or not to drive back to New York. I got into the Audi and pulled out my cell phone. The car, the parking space and the dark garage made a sort of cave, private enough for my tears and railings against life's unforeseen curveballs. Sitting there, I mentally shouted a rebuke to my mother, who had so often repeated the words, "The greatest gift I have given to my children is excellent health and wonderful genes." *Oh please!* I thought.

Who to talk to was the next consideration. I decided that neither daughter needed a call out of the blue with my raw emotion thrust upon them. They would both have enough to deal with eventually as the ramifications of my illness unfolded, if it was, indeed, cancer. Each had a busy and demanding life, neither living close to Bethlehem,

Connecticut. My daughter Philippa had recently moved from Portland, Maine, to Pawtucket, Rhode Island with a brand-new baby girl. Her husband, John, was starting in a new job. She had been struggling with the Maine weather, fatigue and the lack of home care for the baby. My daughter Anastasia had recently returned to London from a job in Hong Kong. She was also busy: embarking on a new life with her boyfriend, Stefan; working full time; and looking for more writing assignments.

I needed to talk with somebody who'd listen and not make me feel they were rushed. Of course, total strangers can come in handy too, but I decided that in a dark garage, late in the afternoon in a city, that wouldn't be such a good choice. And I had no desire to go to a bar, if there were any, on Howard Avenue in New Haven.

Who was one person I really did feel I could count on in my shaky state? Hands down, it was my ex-husband John, still a friend, and sure to be at his farm in Connecticut. I did hesitate for a second, but only a second, as our relationship wasn't always on an even keel. I dialed once but the call failed. That seemed to be a metaphor for my life at the moment.

I dialed again. Hearing John's customary booming "Hello?" I was instantly grateful. My tears—and fears—cascaded out. But terror half-silenced me; all I could manage were stumbling, faltering sentences. The sound of his calm voice consoled me as much as his words. He offered to pick me up, which would have taken him just under two hours, but we decided against it. I could, and would, drive back to the city.

I decided to go to the birthday dinner-dance in New York. In hindsight, the decision to drive back seems crazy after such crippling news, but learned stoicism rose to the fore. Also, I didn't want to miss a beautiful party in a historic old New York building or the celebration of my friend's sixtieth. "Life goes on," I hoped.

Back in New York and in my apartment on East 60th Street, I threw on my clothes. Making up my face, I did my best to conceal the ravages and red eyes of stress before heading across town. My escort for that evening was Stephen Kirschenbaum, in whom I confided. He later said that he'd found me courageous. But then, he is one of those mannerly souls, in addition to being urbane and very witty. We entered the New York Historical Society ballroom, and the bandleader, Peter Duchin, sang "Hello, Dolly" for a couple of lines, inserting my name into the lyrics. It was the first time I'd felt like a person since I'd spoken with Dr. Schwartz.

When the party ended I dropped Stephen off, trekking back across town in a yellow cab. Restless and on edge, I took a hot bath before turning in, but sleep eluded me. "What if" thoughts ran through my brain. What if I hadn't had that telling sonogram? What if I had listened to the residents who had told me not to bother? I remembered ovarian cancer being called the "whispering disease" because there are often no measureable symptoms. Danger signs are vague: bloating, gas or persistent indigestion, a few others which are also not definitive. The only symptoms I had been aware of were fatigue and listlessness. They had been too subtle to act on. I'd ignored them, attributing my discomfort to the fact that I was going through a bad patch in my life.

The next morning, I woke to tepid light filtering through side gaps in my bedroom blinds. As I climbed out of bed, very alone, I was a different woman from the day before. Life would, possibly, never be quite the same again. Dr. Schwartz's words had painted me into a corner with a NO EXIT sign flashing red over my head. If he was right, there was no wiggling out of this one, I thought.

As I made coffee and got the New York Times from the doorstep, I looked around my apartment as if for the first time. Friends during those years told me they had crossed out so many numbers and addresses for me that it was difficult to keep it all straight. Most recently, I had sold a stunning apartment in a very old building, next to the Carlyle Hotel on 76th Street, and used the proceeds to buy two places. My hope had been to organize my life better between city and country, with a small base in New York and a bigger place in Connecticut. This Manhattan apartment was beautiful, its walls patterned in muted red and gold squares by my friend, Rick Jordan, after endless hours of taping. But lovely as it was, the place just wasn't me, partially because the location—way east on 60th street, almost in the river—was very far from my old comfortable part of town. It served only as a chic reminder that I really had no base. The Connecticut house didn't really work either. It, too, was way off the beaten track. I had chosen and devised my own isolation.

Reading the New York Times offered a welcome bit of normalcy. I drank the strong Arabica coffee and browsed the paper, my mind bouncing between denial, the day's news, and terror. *"How could I have done this to myself?" "Maybe it won't be cancer." "I bet it IS cancer." "Will I die?" "Boy, I really dislike what George Bush is doing."*

And then my thoughts focused. I took a deep breath and remembered what the doctor *hadn't* said. He hadn't said I was "riddled" with cancer. That was the way my parents had described friends with the disease back in the 50s—people who always died, it seemed. "Yup, they opened her up, and then closed her right up again. She was riddled with cancer." Dr. Schwartz had said no such thing. He had only said that I had a cyst he suspected was malignant. That difference gave me something to hold on to. For the first time, I faced the fact that there was a lot I could do in preparation for surgery, and began to take action.

I fell into line like a new grunt, soldiering on. Uncompassionate as it seems, information is essential to the business side of processing any illness that requires surgical procedures and a hospital stay, especially an illness requiring large amounts of reimbursement money from the men with the green eye shades and the sharp #3 pencils (or their digital equivalent). Anonymous as a patient may feel being identified by a birth date or case number rather than a name, accurate data greases the wheels of the hospitals and the insurance plans. A wrong middle initial or misspelling can delay a crucial permission from an insurance company, and maybe set back an urgent surgery date.

The first person on my list to see was Dr. John Postley. Frustratingly, it was Saturday, so I would have to wait until Monday to speak to his secretary, Nadine Jean-Baptiste. Nadine always managed to deliver whatever was needed, whether that was a last-minute appointment or a no co-pay MRI. I never doubted her powers of persuasion—a steely hand resides in that velvet glove of hers. Doing all I could for now, I left a message on the office answering service. John Postley knew the family history, had been both mother's and my brother Llewellyn's doctor, and is one of the finest, smartest, doctors anywhere. Grounded and full of common sense, he has a great sense of humor and a positive attitude. He has more information in his little finger about things you want to know about than anyone I have ever been to, as well as a great Rolodex of specialists and the ability to get you in right away to see them.

My mind whirred like a hummingbird's wings as I huddled over a yellow legal pad making a giant list of everything I had to do, trying to prepare for any and all contingencies. Suddenly I remembered what Bobby Lewis, acting guru, had told his students. "Don't postpone. If you have an action or intention, do it now," he would say in a near shout, adding that otherwise distractions set in and the sense of urgency falters. Distraction was inevitable now, but I could try to act. Thinking about who, what, where and when kept my mind off thoughts of "cancer, oh my God." In times of crisis, list-making affords multiple benefits.

What next? Who could I call? I needed to cry again. My pain needed release, with another smart listener who knew me well. There were several possibilities, but I called Susan Kinsolving, a beautiful, funny poet with an understanding of life's dark side. As always, she came through in trumps, predictably solid, deeply intelligent and undaunted by my pain and fear. She clicked right in as I cried, listening with attention and patience to my flood of words. At the end of that conversation, the first of many such we would have in the course of my illness, I felt secure that she and her husband William would help me through. But as I hung up the phone, I shuddered. This was the first time I had ever truly thought about the possibility of dying.

Next, I left a message for Dr. Nancy Lasak, my chiropractor, requesting a Monday appointment. I had long considered a visit to the "bones" doctor an underappreciated insurance policy for preventative medicine, something which prevented blockages and postural problems from getting worse. Chiropractors believe it is essential for patients to take responsibility for their health as best they can. Over many years, Dr. Nancy and I had bonded. Not only did she adjust my body, she adjusted my mind, if need be, and we usually ended up in roars of laughter. She would be an essential member of the team for whatever I was about to go through.

My brain flitting here and there, I had another thought. Two years earlier, a dear friend in London had died of cancer of the liver. It was devastating to watch her go downhill so suddenly. Her death had been calm: sitting up in bed at the London Clinic, smiling and looking angelic in her flannelette Lanz nightie. She passed away just after her husband ordered some fettuccine Alfredo, her favorite dish from her favorite restaurant. He was just telling her about it but she couldn't really hear him and it was sweet, not frightening, but remembering that, I made a different pledge.

My first grandchild, Miranda, was brand new, born just that April, only a couple of weeks before. For a moment, I wondered, "Is she my replacement in nature's birth and death cycle?" Too dramatic, not acceptable, I was *not* ready to be replaced. But the possibility that I would not to watch her grow up, see her milk teeth fall out, discuss the tooth fairy's generosity, get to see her face alter—that prospect rendered me defiant. Dying was not in the cards, I decided, at least not right now.

3

A Snapshot

Humankind cannot bear very much reality.

—T.S. ELIOT

Until I was about eight, old snapshots of me depict a happy and engaged little girl. Though a bit shy, that youngster's face looks bright, as if she is embracing the sun. Later photographs, those yellowed, brittle documents which unveil the past, disclose an unmistakable change. The child in them is now rigid, the face expressionless. She is hard to read. It has taken me over thirty years to figure out why, to learn what it was that changed that little girl and that made her unhappy family "unhappy in its own way," as Tolstoy so perfectly described it.

My family story begins with a mother, the one known to me as Grandma Jeanne: my mother's mother, the only surviving grandparent at the time of my birth. She had been bright, artistic and beautiful, with an artist's bohemian tendencies including her cigarettes, her red wine and later, her Demerol. A singular tragedy—the sort of event my family would see again, if less dramatically—scarred her childhood. She was abandoned by her father. He walked out and took her little brother, Thomas, permanently casting mother and daughter adrift. They never saw him again, though money arrived from Minnesota from time to time. Fortunately, Jeanne and her mother were sheltered by her father's relatives, a kindly, upstanding crew that included two sweet russet-haired spinster schoolteachers and their brother, George. With their support, Jeanne went on to graduate from teacher's college. My mother never spoke of her grandparents, so their history is lost to me.

Skillful childhood eavesdropping revealed this horror story. Jeanne's father's act of betrayal and selfishness sickened me. I wondered how anyone could do such a thing. But I couldn't ask, as I wasn't supposed to know. Grandma Jeanne was the first casualty of abandonment I knew of in my family. But as I would learn, she was hardly the last.

At 19, Jeanne married a man thirty years her senior. Charles Benson, a floor manager in a New York City clothing store, kept her pregnant year after year. A beautiful woman turned into brood mare, Jeanne was trapped in a cramped New York apartment with little help or outlet for her many longings. She performed her wifely duties, producing five healthy children in succession, four sons and a daughter. My mother, Mary Laura Benson, was the third, born in New York City in 1907. About nineteen or twenty years after her marriage, Jeanne left Charles for a dashing Czechoslovakian inventor named Vladimir—a man as passionate for opera, music and art as she was. I suppose her divorce was shocking at the time, but as I pieced together her story, I really couldn't blame her.

Mother rarely discussed her childhood, in fact she avoided it. My guess is there was considerable hardship, caused by the family's lack of money and status and later, war and the Depression. I believe these strained circumstances left her with a bit of a chip on her classy shoulder, helping to create her interest in living well, attaining social position and acquiring wealth which she did through real estate. Like Jeanne, mother was beautiful. But she was also quite insecure and narcissistic. I've often wondered if she might not have been abused or hurt by her brother Frank, a deeply damaged man whose own daughter has referred to close calls and inappropriate behavior. Most often, I found her unapproachable physically and emotionally, both about her own feelings and, later, my own. Yet, she had tremendous charm and we sometimes had a good time together, but there weren't many hugs to be had.

She grew up to become a controlling adult obsessed with 'society' and position. If asked about her childhood, she would fib about having gone to one of the great girls' day schools in New York City, the Spence School, intimating that she then went on to Columbia University. Yet I never glimpsed a school alumnae magazine arrive from either institution, or saw any other proof that she had attended these schools. Risibly flexible with the truth, what she didn't know, mother would just make up. Geraniums became roses, basil could be parsley; the next day the "truth" would change again. At a time when keeping up with the Joneses was an American mantra, she loved the genealogy of her early British and Dutch forebears, some aristocratic, and believed every royal connection noted on the charts she had done by genealogists. Similarly, she emphasized her Southern background, though her forbears penetrated only a few miles south of the Mason-Dixon Line and she grew up in New York City. Mother was proud of joining the Colonial Dames of America, a society whose entrance demanded an officer forbear fighting in the American Revolution, not just any old grunt. (As it happened, he was hit and killed by a thunderbolt on his way into battle!) As I grew up, the most irritating characteristic was the endless obsession with what other people would think, insecurities which paralyzed her at times.

I saw firsthand how important male conquests were to her, along with maintaining her eternally youthful appearance. I often wondered if she considered this quest for youth and beauty her ticket onwards and upwards. On returning from one trip she took to Europe with my father, she boasted that strangers would say they thought she was his daughter, causing me to cringe with embarrassment. She turned her beauty to her advantage, though this was hardly a new or unique approach to female power; perhaps realizing that Jeanne's beauty didn't get her that far in life, I sometimes wondered if she was determined to use hers to ascend further. As I matured, she became competitive with me, further confusing our already complicated relationship. Peace usually demanded submission.

She was rightly proud to have been recruited into the legendary Macy's training program in the late 20s, where she acquired the business and marketing savvy she later turned towards real estate sales in the booming post-war economy of New Canaan, Connecticut. Before my parents married in 1932, mother worked for *Vogue* magazine in New York, where she'd honed her innate fashion sense and style. Possessing grace and gentility, she always emphasized modesty, good manners and civility, abhorred bad language and always described sarcasm as the "lowest form of wit." And she was something of a sidelines feminist, relishing her independence and her successful real estate career. She loved "the art of the deal." Some referred to her as Connecticut's Scarlett O'Hara, though she would have hotly denied Irish blood, not so fashionable in the New Canaan of the 40s. Always in search of an emotional and physical Tara, in her fifties, she finally achieved both.

My father, Llewellyn Ross, was born in Brooklyn in 1897. His father, Edouard Ross, a Frenchman born in Paris, had immigrated to the United States as a youngster. The Ross surname, obviously not French, can probably be attributed to some Scottish mercenary or musket for hire as soldiering was an honorable path out of poverty in rural Scotland. On his mother's side, he was third-generation Irish, his grandfather having settled in Pennsylvania and grown successful.

He went off to World War I at the age of twenty-one, already married, but not to my mother. By the time he married my mother in 1933, he'd been married and twice divorced, once to the beautiful Helen, the butcher's daughter from his Brooklyn neighborhood, and then to a Broadway dancer, name or fame unknown. (I always hoped it might have been Gypsy Rose Lee!) There were no children from either union. Born and raised Catholic but excommunicated through divorce, he could never take Holy Communion, something that affected him deeply.

The cavalry still had horses in World War I, and my father was a cavalry soldier. He sustained serious back injuries—later, he sometimes needed an iron brace when in pain. He was also gassed by the Germans, an experience often given to explain his emotional volatility and explosions of temper although I suspect the seeds of imbalance were in place well before World War I.

When my parents married, he was thirty-six, my mother twelve years younger. After the birth of their first child, my brother, Llewellyn, they moved to New Canaan, then a small New England town of fewer than 5,000 inhabitants. At that time captains of industry, professionals and other successful businesspeople were gravitating towards the town, which was only an hour and ten minutes by train from Grand Central Station. Though close to New York, New Canaan was still 'country,' and the local school system was reputed to be good. The ticket office of the local railroad station still holds a sign that says "New Canaan, the station next to Heaven."

If you had any money in the Depression, a nice house and domestic help were affordable. My parents took advantage of this. They started with Inez and Numa, an African-American couple from Virginia. Next came beloved Lena Luciano, who stayed with our family until her death over forty years later. She came twice a week to clean and do a little cooking. She packed like a dream, using layers of tissue paper to keep my mother's dresses wrinkle-free whenever my parents traveled. Known to us as "Lee Lee," she was both peace maker and pot stirrer. Louise Reed arrived on the scene when I was about eight years old, an additional pair of hands. I loved this woman from Farmville, Virginia like a mother and spent hours in her room talking. Both her fried chicken and apple pie were sublime and I was devastated when she left after my mother remarried. Having inherited some money from his wealthy grandfather, my father started a business in the town combining real estate, travel, and insurance, bringing his Democratic Party values to the staunchly Republican universe of the Fairfield County of the 1930s. He was a man with many interests; reflecting this, his reading material ranged widely, from newspapers and political biographies to the *Reader's Digest* and *Popular Mechanics*.

My parents were bright and aspirational. They fit well in the New Canaan of the 1930s and 40s, though not quite perfectly. One anomaly was that neither had gone to college, my mother's talk of Columbia notwithstanding. My father was more Irish than Scots and hadn't gone to the 'smart' schools, which was a social drawback in New Canaan, where so many of the men had attended Ivy League schools and many of the wives had college degrees. My father pretended not to care, but I believe he did.

At that time, the town was highly stratified. There was little, if any, social integration among its different groups. But we all considered ourselves American, and for most the arrangement seemed to work fairly well. My brothers and I were taught tolerance and to live by the golden rule; we were also taught that everyone is created equal, although I wondered at times if my parents really believed that as I listened in on some of the conversations.

My father stayed active in New York State politics, but ran for Connecticut State Senator in the early 40s, losing roundly to his opponent. To be a Democrat in Fairfield County at that juncture was to be controversial and he was, not everyone loved FDR as he did. More comfortable with the townspeople and his non-WASP buddies than with the country-club set mother pursued, this Brooklyn boy had the quick wit and "common touch" that were always useful for politicians.

Several of my parents' friends were out of the conventional mold, with writers, artists and dancers mixed among the 'smart' set my mother cultivated. I found the conflicts presented by these differences confusing. The well-heeled sent their kids to the Country School, a private day school feeding into East Coast prep schools such as Groton, St. Paul's, and Phillips Andover. In contrast, my brothers and I went through the New Canaan public school system until my brothers reached high school and I reached junior high (as middle school was called then); then we went to boarding schools. I only met the private school kids at the country club during the long summer vacations and at dancing class in the winter. Hardly any of the other public school kids belonged to the country club, which added to my sense of not knowing where, exactly, I belonged.

Over the years my father's business expanded, as did the family. There were now three children, two older boys and me, "the baby." In 1942, we moved on to a bigger, better house in a nicer part of town. Dennis, Llewellyn and I spent most of our childhood in a picture-book New England farmhouse. It had a big apple orchard on one side and a huge red barn that held scary bats, a deteriorating rosewood piano and some rusty farm machinery on the other. I can remember, at three, running down to the barn with my mother to collect eggs from the hens we kept during the war.

There was a lot of outdoor space to explore, too. We had a big wartime victory garden tended by Butch, a lovely Italian with a bright smile and a memorable gold tooth in front. Mother and Lena would put up its produce for the winter, lining the shelves of the cellar larder with labeled Mason jars full of plum tomatoes, applesauce and beans. A short walk away, there was a pond with water moccasins, snapping turtles and frogs. A huge empty field lay in front of the house. As an eleven-year-old, I dinged the family station wagon there, egged into practicing driving by my middle brother, Dennis, while our parents were away.

It was real country with more bees, birds and wildlife than I see today in the outdoors. Honeysuckle scented the summer air down by the barn as I practiced hitting tennis balls on its dusty red side. Mary and Llewellyn Ross were handsome folk and we seemed to have all the trappings of the American dream. Weren't we lucky!

Yet something was missing. Behind closed doors in that quaint, charming New England farmhouse, my parents were growing in different directions, becoming two increasingly dissatisfied malcontents locked in a steadily more difficult, contentious marriage. As time passed, the tensions became clear to all. Even then, I understood how different they were. But three children and a mortgage—and perhaps my father's fear of a fourth marriage—bonded them together. As so many did at the time, they toughed it out. So did the children, and therein lies the tale.

Our young lives were shaped by ill-defined boundaries, inconsistent parenting, occasional violent discipline, and withheld love. None of the three of us knew that language, but we experienced the reality behind the words and no one escaped without scarring. The energy in the house felt acrid much of the time, amid my father's outbursts and my mother's back-biting. We never got to experience what a truly loving relationship was like. Additionally, the relationship between my mother and middle brother was so strong that I used to think of them almost as a couple. Many years later, I was shocked when a therapist called this "spiritual incest." But the term was apt. The fact that he was always favored in our childhood roughhousing became painfully obvious to me.

And so, understanding this with only a child's emotional vocabulary, I went from that bright and happy child to the girl who photographed as withdrawn. If memory serves, it was at about eleven or twelve years old that the phrase, "I must break the chain, I must break the chain" started repeating in my head, desperate to be heard. I had no idea why I was thinking those words. I only knew "the chain" somehow referred to our circumstances, my parents' behavior, the family's collective past– and those tales of loss and abandonment I had stored and which eddied through my inner life. Affected by my parents' relationship, I felt a heaviness of spirit infect the atmosphere, a sadness from which I was unable to free myself. Dissension became the primary color, the air I seemed to breathe. Like most kids, I just wanted everyone to be happy; somehow, I began to feel responsible. We are all storytellers; tales of our families and forebears are crucial to our identity. My child's mind sought better stories.

I'm not exactly sure when the nightmares started, but it was around this time. They remained constant in my life from my teens until they mostly ceased about ten years ago. Both of my husbands bore witness to these upheavals, which made them feel upset and helpless. I had no definitive answers for them. My own screams would wake me up. I was never able to figure out exactly what was so upsetting. The only constants were my father as part of the *mise-en-scène* and flashbacks of going for a swim with him. I could pinpoint the location of the dream, a beach club the family belonged to on Long Island Sound. But it took many years and much therapy to reach that point of readiness where I could deal with the real subject of these recurrent nightmares. Finally, I was able to piece together the puzzle, but not without a long and arduous struggle and help from a surprising quarter.

Here is what I finally remembered. It was the dog days of August in Connecticut. My father, who worked in town, had come home early. He asked me if I'd like to go for a swim at the beach club. It was the annual summer vacation. The trip sounded like a nice way to cool off and maybe wheedle an ice cream.

It was low tide when we arrived at the beach club. I remember thinking that I'd be able to dig for a clam, using my feet to search in the squishy, satisfying low-tide muck. My father and I walked through the almost empty club and up the stairs to the second floor, towards the family changing locker. I don't remember whether my father asked me to come in with him or if he went in first and then invited me to enter; I believe the former.

On alert for some reason, I initially said, "No, Daddy." But ultimately I did go in. What I so long repressed was a memory of my father having me touch him sexually. I don't remember anything else that happened, except that he then left.

I changed, slowly. Then I remember walking out on the jetty, silently, to swim. I felt as if I had turned all white and bloodless. I remember noticing that my father had some red marks on his fat stomach, and feeling sad for him. We didn't speak during the swim; I stayed as far away from him as I could. Nothing more about that day remains in my memory. I must have been around twelve years old.

For years, I've struggled to accept this memory. To this day, I still wonder if my mind has played tricks on me, and if what I remember is the exact truth or a subjective recreation. Whichever it is, I do know that on that day, something happened that seriously affected my life, and that my father had something to do with it.

Life continued uneventfully, if also uneasily, for a while. Two years later, during the intensely hot and languid August of 1955, I got my first period and my first bra. Having both seemed like quite an achievement. All I really knew about menstruation came from an older friend who would talk about blood "down there" and "the curse." This was the pre-pill, pre-Haight-Ashbury, pre-computer era. I didn't suspect very much at all; I certainly didn't know I'd already lost some part of my innocence.

Later that same month, my father and mother arrived home early one evening after a meeting of travel agents. I remember my father was eating a vanilla Dairy Queen cone, despite his diabetes. That night, he suffered a major coronary thrombosis. Mother rushed into my room, screaming, "Your father is dying! Your father is dying! Get up!" Startled, I rose and went to sit with my brothers through this unfolding drama. Dr. Hebard, the family doctor, arrived soon after the attack. Leaving after his examination, he paused to say our father did not have long to live, and that he would return in the morning.

I could hear my father moaning as we sat our vigil and waited through the night. He did die, early the next morning. My mother was in and out of his room; I guess she sat with us, too, but I mostly remember my brother, Llewellyn, and the sound of Louise sobbing in her quarters. It was all so fast and dramatic that I went onto a sort of automatic pilot, I guess, stunned and traumatized.

I never saw my father's face again, alive or dead; when his beloved town firemen came to remove his body, he left on a stretcher, completely covered. A couple of them had tears in their eyes as he was loved and respected by many of these local men, having initiated a special pension plan for them.

4

Unchained Dissonance

The cruelest lies are often told in silence.
— ROBERT LOUIS STEVENSON

After his death, my father was hardly mentioned. Louise, Lena and I were the only ones who talked about him. This was still the era of sweeping unpleasantness under the rug, and grief counseling didn't yet exist. Each of us seemed to be fending for ourselves; thoughts were kept private. My older brother, Llewellyn, was willing to drop out of Princeton, but mother insisted he stay; he paid some of his expenses by modeling for the New York Times and other men's fashion supplements. Dennis, never a student, joined the Air Force at seventeen after escorting my mother on a couple of trips to Europe.

A few years ago, Llewellyn told me he believed our parents had been on the verge of separating at the time of our father's death. I was unaware of it but he was most likely having an affair with a recently widowed Englishwoman who lived in town. Not pretty, she was intelligent, had a bawdy sense of humor and didn't mind a drink. I didn't understand his trips with her back then, or question them too deeply. Possibly my subconscious had already figured it out. This was not my father's only "friendship" with a woman. One had ended in a fistfight with an angry husband at a cocktail party, an episode which I believe was the final knife through my mother's heart. After that, I think any sense of marital trust or intimacy was completely over for her.

So with my father's death came the scattering of the family. The death, confusion and dispersal threw me into a depression, which lasted for about seven years. Wary as I had been of him, my father had been the one to praise my schoolwork and other small achievements; bright and charismatic, he was the parent I felt closer to. The year after his death, my grades plummeted from high honors to almost failing scores, and that lackluster performance continued throughout my early academic life. Much later, through therapy, I began to understand that the reasons for my low spirits and confusion were far more complex, and included other problems in addition to his sudden death.

My mother would remarry two more times. The first of these marriages, made within a year after my father's death, was to a man remarkably unsuitable for her, especially considering her social ambitions. It unwound quickly. As the union disintegrated, she claimed to be in a weakened state, disabled by her menstrual problems; she, too, had a cyst, hers in her uterus.

My relationship with her was complex even in those years. Though she played the innocent, she nevertheless tried hard to influence my friendships. She didn't succeed, but her meddling added to the mix of my inner chaos. I caught her opening my mail and listening to telephone conversations. She always had a lot to say about people's backgrounds, her 'three Bs' being 'beauty, brains and breeding.' *Ha*, I would think, *so much for tolerance!* But she had become all I had, so I suppressed my feelings of rebellion. At times I loved her very much, had fun with her and enjoyed her company. But often, I felt more like the mother and not the child. She found me amusing and smart. Much as I felt sorry for her, I found her impenetrable, a brick wall who seemed capable only of commenting on my haircut or the color of my dress. As I look back, I can see there were deep misunderstandings on both sides and that she was struggling, also.

My mother didn't exactly program me for marriage, but let's just say that continuing my education was not high on her list of priorities. My dreams of joining the Peace Corps were shot down, my wish to become a photographer subtly ridiculed. Until the day she started vamping my boyfriends, I mostly wished her well. A couple of my youthful romances saw through her egoistic flirtations. But I felt humiliated by her commands, her power plays. "Betsy, bring me my glasses" or "Get me a pillow," she would dictate, often in front of others. These were my Cinderella years, a time of slow, incinerating rage.

One of the funnier efforts during these years was mother's attempt to charm the headmaster of the Foxcroft School into accepting me for admission just three weeks before the September 1957-58 school year began. This was a project doomed from the start. Foxcroft was, and is, one of the most socially desirable girls' boarding schools in the country; in spite of her clothes, her fancy Mercedes and her charm, my mother could not twist the arm of its headmaster. Undaunted by rejection, at the very last moment she managed to get me into a girl's *pensionnat*, a boarding school, in Lausanne, Switzerland. This move was mostly designed to build our social rank (to speak French conveyed great status, a third language even more) and to remove me from yet another disintegrating marital situation. But it did involve good intentions, and the idea of spending a year in Europe thrilled me. With characteristically mixed motives, my mother allowed me to have a very special experience, one for which I am eternally grateful.

My year at the *Ecole Brillantmont* turned out to be stellar, a boost in every way. Not only did I acquire passable French with a good accent, but I learned to ski, winning a championship for all the boarding school beginners and falling in love with the mountains. At the same time, I developed a lasting love of Europe, of Switzerland and of dark chocolate.

The first few weeks of school, I was terribly homesick. I cried so much that the headmistress contacted my mother to bring me home. Then, a sea change occurred. I made a friend from the States who was also homesick. I found myself in a house on the campus with girls from seven different countries, all far from home, who were fun, naughty and supportive. All of a sudden I settled in.

Mostly though, it was the headmistress, Mademoiselle Heubi, the school founder's daughter, who made the difference. Well into her eighties, she stood at the entrance to the dining room each night as we exited and looked deeply into our eyes as she firmly shook our hands to say, "Bonsoir." There was something so profoundly kind and wise in that blue-eyed, probing gaze that I felt cared for. When my mother said Mademoiselle Heubi had called her about me, something changed. From then on I wanted to stay. Later, "Wuss," who you'll meet in a minute, gave me more maternal surrogacy. But something ever more profound was affecting me. In all my dealings, especially with the school and Wuss, I was being fairly dealt with and this, ultimately, would reinstate my wavering belief in human goodness and kindness.

The original plan was for me to go back home for Christmas. Then my American friend, Patsy Parker, invited me to join her over the long Christmas break on a skiing holiday in Engelberg, a small, charming Swiss-German skiing resort. Having been so terribly homesick, I now wanted nothing more than to stay over the holiday, so I did, surprising those at home.

The chaperone would be Patsy's mother's former English governess, the extraordinary Elsie Slade, also known as "Wuss." Vibrant but tiny, in her eighties, Wuss turned out to be everything I needed. Guide, friend and mentor, she was nonjudgmental and unrelentingly reassuring. Her virtuous character shone, reflected in everything from her highly shined, sensible brown walking shoes to the soft but rakish tweed hat resting gently on her grey hair. Gently nurturing, at the same time encouraging fun, she expected fairness and good behavior. Having had a career in dealing with other people's children, Wuss must have picked up on my unhappiness and struggles. Seeing a spirit in torment, she gave that needed extra support and love. In my treasure chest of heroes and heroines, Wuss reigns supreme, helping me to trust once more those in authority.

Back at home, things were changing. Louise, my longtime surrogate mom, quit shortly after mother remarried, marrying her own Mr. Lawrence, pillar of the Baptist Church. Loathing mother's new husband on sight, she wanted out. I'm not sure how mother felt about her at that time, but in any case, she was suddenly gone.

My antagonistic, conflicted feelings against my mother were growing steadily worse. I tried to remain loyal, but we were on a straight collision course. Back from Switzerland, I became a boarder for the final year at my old school, Rosemary Hall. Mother was often away, newly divorced and traveling, adding to my sense that my family foundation, never very strong, was crumbling further. Again, a special woman stepped in. The late Mary Ward, the mother of a school friend, took me under her family's wing. She not only cared for me in the Ward home when I became sick with mumps, but gave me a deep sense of being welcome and included. She was a petite, passionate, fiercely loyal and outspoken lady who did not hold back with her opinions, even when it came to making me aware of her lack of respect for my mother. I know this was out of a genuine concern for my development. It will always be an honor to call this fabulous woman, with her compassion and love of truth, both friend and mentor.

My father had left his finances and estate in a mess. He had made some poor business decisions, funding ventures including a hair straightener for people of color. (Poor Louise was the guinea pig for that one. One morning, she arrived in the kitchen, her uniform and apron crisp and white, clumps of hair gripped in her hand; the aftermath of a 'Strair' treatment, its name short for straight hair.) That and other investments had become family jokes, but the family assets had been seriously dwindling. Now, coming home from school on weekends, I always found the same pile of unpaid bills on the dining room table. Bright with glaring 'Overdue' stickers, they waited for mother's signature on checks to pay them off, but those checks were not forthcoming.

Although only pulling in mediocre grades, I wanted to go to college. That May I was pleased to have been accepted by Briarcliff, a women's junior college, now defunct. The headmistress of my school, Miss McBee, was disappointed. I should and could have achieved much more, she said, having no idea of the family circumstances, unable to pierce my armor. My expectations had been low, I suppose.

At Briarcliff, the dodgy, detached academic performance continued. I was consistently bluffing my way through, always postponing, never able to concentrate. Only through rereading my transcript did I rediscover what my courses had been. During this time, a Princeton contemporary of my brother's, much older, came into my life. He stayed there for several years, until my Mother pressured him to leave me alone. I was too young to make a decision and he was too old, said she. The truth is that he was pretty immature, too.

Meanwhile, her life expanded. Grandma Jeanne had died and not long after mother bought both a lease on a fancy Belgravia apartment and a travel business in London, giving the job of running it to the man who would become husband number three, Edgar. This transatlantic courtship was in progress during the 1960 school year. I was discouraged from using the house in Connecticut, as she wished it "closed." Therefore, I had no real home base for that last year in college. I spent free weekends with a family friend who was nice enough to take me in, a lively septuagenarian who seemed happy to have company. By this point I was "bringing myself up", but I often needed to seek out a landing pad or surrogacy on the uneven path to becoming an adult. Like a homing pigeon I always returned to New Canaan, always seeking, always attempting to forge some connection with my roots, even notionally.

After Briarcliff, as mother was still away, I stayed for a time with my brother and his wife in Cincinnati. After they had given me emotional support for several months, it became time to move on. One Sunday morning in Cincinnati, reading the paper, I read about a Pan-American Airways program known as Flight 1. It went around the world, allowing ticketed passengers to make as many stops as they wanted, then pick it up again. Surprisingly, it wasn't that expensive. My time in Europe had given me a travel bug, and I had no real place to live. I took the remaining money from a small trust fund and persuaded Carina, my septuagenarian friend, we should go together. The two of us set off for an eighty-day trip around the world. Carina referred to us as May and December, yet we had fun together despite that great age difference. An early graduate of the Yale School of Architecture, she was knowledgeable about world architecture and art, fearless at networking, and blessed with acquaintances all over the world. I learned a lot about all these things as we touched down in world capitals from Bagdad to Bombay to Bangkok.

Returning home, I moved in with a college friend in New York City. After a short stint in public relations, I landed a job at *Harper's Bazaar* magazine. It was an exciting time, with great photographers like Richard Avedon and Francesco Scavullo doing fashion; the atmosphere of monthly magazines is highly energized and energizing. I stayed for three years, loving the fashion but not so much the task of dealing with difficult, ambitious women. That struck too close to the bone. I moved on to Sotheby's, where I worked in the painting department as what might have been the worst secretary they ever had. I loved having the chance to go down the racks of impending sales pictures and select a little Picasso or Modigliani to hang over my desk until it was needed for auction. My dream of becoming a photographer had been placed on the back burner, but I still held that idea, stimulated by all the work at the *Bazaar* as well as the constant flow of art in my daily life.

By that time, I had a new boyfriend. He was another older man, this time by sixteen years, a divorcée with four young children. Jimmy was the most romantic and sophisticated of any boyfriend I had ever had. But I was both too immature and not enough in love to commit to marriage. The idea of becoming a stepmother when I needed a mother myself was too overwhelming. More important, I had met the man I *would* marry.

Looking back, I see myself as unfocused and angry. But I could put on a good front. I loved the freedom and independence I had in New York, the new people, the excitement and the buzz. If not quite *Sex and the City*, it was thrilling, from Warhol and the Factory to the lively theatre and Pop art scenes, the excitement of work and many parties. Some of my unhappiness seemed to be passing. I felt cared for. Moving to my own apartment, I made new friends, and was beginning to find myself, but not without some help.

A friend was in treatment with a European psychologist named Sigfrid von Koch. Dr. von Koch was tall and aristocratic, with wiggly, bushy eyebrows and a lit cigarette always attached to his ubiquitous Dunhill cigarette holder, the kind with filters you had to change. My love life was getting complicated, I was confused about Jimmy, the nightmares continued, and I was beginning to understand the by-products of my mother's effect on me. It felt like the right time for some counseling.

From the first appointment, I could see this doctor understood my background and the kind of place I came from. Sitting and facing each other, both in an identical brown leather banquette, we talked and smoked, Pinteresque pauses underscoring our dialogue. I learned to be careful when stamping out my cigarettes—he claimed to be able to tell a lot about a person by the way they did so. We exhumed my parents' marriage, examined my relationship with them and my brothers, spoke of the shock of my father's death and of how I perceived him. I told the doctor that I had been fond of my father, but wary. I talked about the nightmares where my father continued to be a presence. He requested that I write down the details of any of my subsequent dreams.

Dr. von Koch placed great stock on dream analysis. Once we had developed a weekly appointment, I would keep pad and pencil by my bed the night before and pray for a really good dream. Usually I produced one, including reruns of the standby nightmare. The doctor probed around the possibility of sexual malfeasance by my father. Uncomfortable, I continued to skirt the issue. I've worked with several therapists over the years, and I would say all have had suspicions of abuse. I was not yet ready to fully discuss my father. But with Dr. von Koch's help, I built self-esteem and a better sense of my identity, gaining courage and learning more about my anger.

The work made me feel stronger; my knowledge of boundaries strengthened. Suddenly I could stand up to my mother, less scared of abandonment. My new energy had force and when I let go, it wasn't always pleasant. His eyebrows wiggling and Prussian-blue eyes flashing, von Koch said, "You used to be afraid to say 'boo' to a goose. That's no longer the case." It was no surprise that relations with my mother were not improving. My new step-father, Edgar, became an ally, and as mother didn't want to appear unkind, she had to rein herself in. Edgar's gentlemanly qualities and essential fairness worked in my favor. He could see both sides of a story and mediate without seemingly showing favoritism, a great gift.

5

Tying the Knot

Let the winds of the heavens dance between you.
— Kahil Gibran

At 25, almost 26, after a short courtship and engagement, I married the man who would father my two daughters. A handsome, cultivated and bright man, Hilary loved and had lived in Vietnam and Paris, "the city of lights," where he lives to this day. Though he was shy, there was something very special about this cultivated Harvard boy from Oklahoma who reminded me of Jack Kennedy, loved French movies, and smoked Gauloises cigarettes down to the butt end. Our wedding was beautiful despite all-out warfare with mother regarding every detail, from the print color of the invitation to the choice of music, a trio of Russian musicians with waltzing violins and red cummerbunds. I won both those rounds.

The interest in physical well-being I'd honed in Switzerland continued during my New York working life. My new husband was a dedicated walker, and we strolled together all over the city on our way to and from movies or a quick dinner out. I had joined a gym in New York owned and run by Nicholas Kounovsky, a White Russian, formerly of Paris. His gym attracted many of the "beautiful people", as Diana Vreeland dubbed them in the 60s, especially the models. I was no model, but I'd done yoga, tried acupuncture and liked Swedish massage. As a "fashionista," looking good was of interest, too. Sometimes I'd sneak over to Kounovsky's studio at lunch break to do the trapeze work and calisthenics. My father's excess weight and lack of exercise had made an impression; besides, it was obvious that the beautiful people were not overweight and had a lot of energy.

Kounovsky was interesting. He had studied aeronautics and trained as a gymnast. Using this knowledge of both engineering and exercise, he had devised a system of gymnastics that he called "sixometry," which focused on six basic elements necessary for fitness: endurance, suppleness, balance, strength, speed, and skill (or coordination). Kounovsky stressed that each of the six should have equal time. He believed that standing on one's head in a three-point balance of head and arms could perfect equilibrium. Before my pregnancy in 1967, we worked out on mats, trapezes, rings and parallel bars. Once I was pregnant the routine was gentler, with more stretching but still rigorous enough to feel like boot camp.

After marriage, I kept up the visits. Anastasia was born in minutes, a blessing which I attribute to those workouts. I breast-fed for about four months but not all the joys and skills of parenting came easily for me. I was a bit scared of implementing some of the natural cooking ideas, like giving the baby the vegetable water to drink. I never knew whether or not to pick up the baby or let her cry as various books suggested. I mostly followed Dr. Spock's instructions, and not wanting her to cry, I usually picked her up. Frankly, I was overwhelmed to be married, to have had a baby right away, and to be with someone who was working very late hours (and still working when he returned home). I was getting depressed again and did not feel confident to have such huge responsibilities.

Nevertheless, not only did we move to London within six months after Anastasia's birth, but our marriage produced another child within 30 months, a beautiful little girl. Philippa was born seven weeks premature, which was unnerving for several reasons. She developed jaundice a few days after her birth, and briefly, the outcome was uncertain. She had to remain in an incubator at the hospital for weeks. I tried hard and was sorry not to breastfeed her, too, but she weighed only four and half pounds at birth and couldn't suck, while my body was not ready to produce milk. Her father and I were not happy, either. I figured that she had been too smart to stay in an unhappy womb, and having picked up on the restlessness within me, decided to make her entrance a bit early.

She was so little when she got home, I felt inadequate. I relied on the assistance of an excellent mother's helper, Kathy, who was well-trained in Switzerland and who stayed for almost two years, until Philippa was walking and talking and I felt more secure with her. Then we had a stream of *au pairs*. I was not a good 'picker.' The girls can tell stories about them, including one named Marie-José who was apparently producing a Basque separatist newspaper out of our tiny flat. They claim she had a pistol underneath her bed along with the printing press. But I am rushing ahead. Unfortunately, by the time Philippa appeared, our marriage was in big trouble.

In retrospect, I think that one set of insecurities had attracted the other's, like water seeking its own level. Six years later, we divorced. Hilary moved to Paris, while part of our divorce agreement stipulated that I stay on in London. That worked, although imperfectly. The girls had begun a school which they seemed to like and in which they were doing well. I found a charming, rooftop flat, affordable and within walking distance of the school. Too uncertain and financially unstable to move back to New York, I stayed in London, a city I loved. Besides, according to Hilary's terms, I was not allowed to go back to the States. In any case I didn't want to be that close to, or dependent on, my mother.

As the girls were now both in school full time, I could work. I finally became the photographer I had wished to become. I nabbed a job covering events for British *Vogue*, as well as working for other magazines as a freelancer and assisting in other photographer's studios. A new man came along, divorced and charming. He loved my girls, missed his own children in California, and for three or four years we were a couple. The romance ended, but the friendship didn't.

Harry gave us a lot of the loving support we needed; it almost felt like a family, at least on the weekends. I was deeply saddened by his untimely death at the age of 50. The summer Harry died I contracted hepatitis, leaving me weak. The three or four year period after the divorce had produced several small and not-so-small illnesses, not just the hepatitis but also bad flus and colds.

Then, I met John, tall and handsome, funny and smart. He had known my brother, Llewellyn. I had heard stories about him. He had bushy eyebrows like Dr. von Koch and beautiful, kind blue eyes with a hint of lavender in them. There was an instant spark between us. I could tell he was more than nice; I could tell he was a great example of the best kind of American male with unassailable family values. He loved to cook and to shop for wonderful food. He adored antiques and knew the best florist in London. He had three boys, mostly grown up, and lots of friends. Over a short period, we fell in love. I was hooked. My ten years on my own ended. We married in 1986 in New York City, Mother hurling the rose petals and rice with that glint in her eye. With that, my full-time life in London ended.

I was 45 at this time. My ovarian cyst made its debut around then, coinciding with perimenopause. The synthetic estrogen and progestin supplement Prempro was recommended and prescribed. It was considered a wonder drug, the gold standard of its time, and freely dispensed by gynecologists everywhere. I took it for many years—too many, I believe, as it turned out.

John was still working. Photography no longer interested me that much; my ultimate job at Town and Country had been in sales, which really didn't interest me. With time on my hands, I began to take acting classes. I studied first with Earle Hyman, recognizable as the grandfather on Bill Cosby's show, then with the legendary Robert Lewis, one of the founders of the Actor's Studio. I even had some classes with the late Stella Adler. In the studio system at MGM in Hollywood, said Bobby, the actors studied everything: dancing, singing, fencing, and movement, so I began to do all those things, too. It was catch-up time for me.

Acting is a way to learn more about yourself—that is, if you are ready to be very honest. To find the character within and release emotion through using your own experiences is part of what acting technique is about. In scene study, you have to find the intention of your character, what he or she wants as that relates to the entire play. In Bobby's view, everybody wants the same thing in different forms, and it's the actor's job to convey it.

If you can't access those deeper parts, using your experience and imagination truthfully, you don't progress. Blunted, with a lot of feelings submerged, I had a very hard time learning to do that. There were places I was fearful to go. But I persevered. Finally, something began to rise up like lava. It helped that I was living with someone I trusted, though he didn't like the time I was devoting to this pursuit. These classes morphed into a rebirth. The energy and feelings released were not easy for either John or me to deal with. Huge releases of unfocused anger were part of the package; at times, I really didn't know what was happening. It wasn't exactly what John had in mind, newly wedded to a nice girl from New Canaan. Having just shepherded three boys through their adolescence, he was not looking for more of the same kind of drama from me.

I don't think I was totally at fault, but I could readily see my contribution to our problems. Beyond the acting, having lived on my own for ten of the last twenty years, and experiencing a different way of life in England made my re-entry more challenging than I had anticipated. I was very happy to be nearer my girls, now at school in America, but I was returning to a way of life which I had partly rejected by leaving it.

I had scores of questions. Was history, I wondered, rearing its ugly head? Was I repeating my mother's and father's history with different packaging? Was this just about commitment? What the hell was going on here?

Dr. von Koch had died by then. I found a new, smart and hip psychiatrist. When the conversation turned to my father, the doctor had many questions. "Did your father work in town, or did he commute to New York?" "Did your father wear a dressing gown or bathrobe around the house with no clothes under it?" "Did he drink alcohol, and if so, was it every day?"

The answers were "yes, yes" and "yes." My father had worked New Canaan, he wore bathrobes at home with no clothes underneath as far as I could remember, and he drank every day. (To be fair, many people drank every day.) Alcoholics and alcoholism being one of this physician's specialties, he knew what he was asking about. I believe he was the first person to actually say he was convinced I had been sexually abused by my father.

The next was a homeopathic MD in Woodbury, Connecticut. Taking a long history, an important part of a homeopath's examination, she learned that I'd experienced persistent nightmares for many years, and liked to keep my bedroom doors closed (a paranoia remarked upon by John, the most normal of men). "It sounds to me as if you were sexually abused and don't realize it," the doctor announced, adding there were more signs of it in my story than she usually heard in these cases. My reaction to this assessment was a bit strange. I wasn't that shaken by what she said. It was almost as if my unconscious was saying, "Yes, I am beginning to think that, too."

Realizing that we weren't going to make it, John and I separated after five years, sorting things out amicably. Our relationship contractually ended after a few failed attempts to reunite, but it was never really over. Something good was always circulating in the ether, though it took many years to bring us together again.

There were extended periods of being together, not together, and not really knowing what we were doing. As we lived a civilized but accessible distance from each other, we got together for dinner from time to time. During this chapter of my life, I had a house in Roxbury, Connecticut. I met many locals including a very interesting psychologist. Phyllis Beauvais conducted her practice in her barn in Roxbury, Connecticut. She and her husband ran a kind of rehab and home for seriously troubled kids, usually from the inner city. Expert on abuse of all kinds, she had developed many different ways to get her often wily and unwilling patients to talk.

One day towards the end of a session, she asked if I would like to do "screaming therapy." I trusted Phyllis so, curious, I gamely took the two velvet cushions offered and waited for instructions. Suggesting I hold them close to my body, Phyllis said that I should start by just beating them, thinking of whatever came to mind, not editing and getting rough with the cushions if I wanted to.

To my utter surprise, after a minute or so I started yelling something like "I hate you. I hate you, damn you," After several minutes, I was on the floor, knees tucked under my body, exhausted. Seconds later, I found myself saying to the space in front of me, "Oh Daddy, no, it can't be." And that was it. A new pathway had carved its way through my deepest self, the beginning of an exploration that would eventually help me accept a destructive reality which was very sad to acknowledge. Having lived with the suggestions, the nightmares, and the veiled locker-room memories for such a long time, this outburst was from a place far deeper than any suggestion or talk might reach. Held for so long in my body, it had risen up from the soul itself.

My nightmares diminished somewhat. When they recurred, they contained more information and detail, less concealment. This part of my journey coincided with a number of celebrities revealing abuse in their lives, Barbra Streisand and Roseanne Barr among them. Needing to be absolutely certain about this possibility of abuse, I pulled back. Still, my need for closure gathered strength and energy. As I read about different consequences of abuse, I realized how much of the maladaptive behavior described seemed to fit me and my life experiences.

Meanwhile, my separation from John was disappointing to all, including my children, who were close to him. It's still hard for me to realize how messed up I was. I was trying so hard to make the right choices, and thought I'd seen the back of a lot of problems. I had, but there was still much to be done.

Therapy is great for understanding events intellectually. Repeated sessions can help a patient accept reality, but I have learned that that the *body* must physically experience the release of emotion—that the intersection of mind, spirit and body has to happen. I had been told that the "spirit is sneaky." When ready, it appears, and helps us if we'll let it.

From an unusual quarter—dentistry—a breakthrough occurred. I was taking singing lessons as part of my acting work. To sing well, you have to breathe without tension and be able to remain centered and grounded, neither of which I was good at. It was easy to push me off my feet. My jaw was like steel, hard to release and rigid. My singing teacher, the late Marianne Challis, said it was preventing my flow of breath; she gave exercises and suggestions to help, but they were never enough. The endless body work I did to stay limber didn't help either. Finally, my chiropractor suggested I see Dr. Michael Gelb. His specialty was TMJ, temporomandibular joint disorder, more commonly known as tight jaw.

I had my appointment with the doctor and was fitted for a mouth guard, something many people have. But this one was different, constructed in such a way as to release my lower jaw and its muscles during sleep. After wearing the mouth guard at night for about two weeks, I began to get very clear images of the locker-room episode, becoming extremely agitated.

It was essential to see Dr. Gelb immediately although it was a month before our next appointment. I had to ask him if others had come back with a similar story. I made the date and waited anxiously in the dental chair on the appointed day. Floored when he told me it was not totally unusual to have a patient come back with these kinds of remembrances, I burst into tears. Stunned and grateful, I felt somehow vindicated. From then on, the nightmares almost, but not totally, stopped. But I still maintained a degree, although lessened, of denial and doubt. How would I ever know for certain? Now, many years later, I have an answer to that question: I don't know for certain. I may always have a sense of confusion about exactly what happened. But as

I've said before, I do know that something happened with my father that altered my psyche and my life.

Frustrated, one of my goals became to finally figure out what it really takes to have a good relationship, and see if I could ever qualify. Returning to a marriage counselor John and I had seen together, I worked on it with no holds barred, trying to understand as much as I could about the elements of my past that were getting in my way. During one of the sessions, I mentioned the abuse issue and my perpetual discomfort in accepting it. Mimi Renschmer, the therapist, understood my distress. She declared that if you see images in dreams, or awake, and they recur over decades, then you can trust that the event did happen. With those words, I had the "eureka" moment, finally accepting my memory as true. The dreams ceased immediately. I have experienced only two or three since in the intervening years.

Later I would read Candace Pert's book *The Molecules of Emotion*, which asserts that the body itself stores emotion, not just the mind. She speaks of stress causing cellular changes. "Children and adolescents who are exposed to stressful situations show a wide range of complex reactions which may be immediate or delayed," she writes. "Their reactions are age-dependent and strongly influenced by the action of the adults with whom they come into contact, especially their 'care-givers.' " In other words, early trauma can create not just emotional but physical changes. In my own life, my belief is that cellular stress at an early age, created by sexual abuse among other family issues, had forced me to live with my sympathetic nervous system on red alert, always gearing up for "fight or flight."

With the body work, talk therapy, and life experience all converging, I was slowly beginning to recognize that my rocky early emotional life was powerfully affecting my body. Yet I believed I'd done almost all of the repair work necessary to fix my life. I certainly had worked on it for long enough to sort out the main segments. Or so I thought.

Then came the diagnosis.

6

Waving, not Drowning

Always remember, the future comes one day at a time.

— DEAN ACHESON

One thing was clear: I would need at least one second opinion, maybe more. Too often in the past I had taken things at face value, only to discover that my reaction had been too hasty or my agreement with someone else's suggestion too quick. This time the stakes could not have been higher, so I knew a second opinion would be critical. I had to make certain the Yale decision was the right decision. Besides, it is simple common sense to do so, and I felt a fighting energy and focus, elusive in recent months.

Dr. Schwartz had been very clear that I had choices, but with one crucial exception. If the tumor was cancerous, the only option would be removal of all my reproductive organs, a complete hysterectomy. He had even discussed whether the incision should go lengthwise or across the width of my abdomen. "Do you wear a bikini?" he had asked, a sweet question under the circumstances. I told him I occasionally wore one when I had the guts to do it.

Puzzling over the problem of whom to consult, I had considerable cannon fodder for this quest. In New York City, I knew people and people who knew people if I didn't. Paul Marx, former head of

Memorial Sloan-Kettering Hospital, was a friend of friends and I had once or twice met him socially. Formerly hesitant to ask favors of acquaintances, I was now in a ballgame with different rules. Memorial Sloan-Kettering would be geographically more convenient than Yale. More importantly, it was one of the finest cancer hospitals in the world. I left a message for Dr. Marx at his house in Connecticut, hearing my mother's voice tuned in from eternity's airwaves. "Always go to the top, dear," vibrated in my ear. In the past, I'd found her star turns embarrassing, but now I thought they were great. I seized on to them like a Rottweiler, trying to remember what she did and how she did it. I found myself laughing as I remembered her calls to Jack Welch, then CEO of General Electric, who had been her next-door neighbor. Her freezer kept breaking down and she'd coyly suggest he might send someone over to look at it. A sporting man, he always obliged, though I doubt hers was even a GE appliance.

What I still hadn't done was telephone my daughters. That was an intentional decision. I had needed time to get a grip on myself and figure out what to say. For years I had struggled with chronic guilt. I believed that I'd let them down by divorcing their father when they were so very young, and then again by staying on in London when they were at boarding school in the States, although I had no choice. But I so needed to make sure this was well handled, mindful of their circumstances. Philippa's husband John's father was dying of cancer, adding to her exhaustion. As I said above, Anastasia, too, was very busy.

Both of them were good at reading my voice so I needed to sound stronger than I possibly felt. I called, reaching them both in turn. I gave them the news in a matter-of-fact way, emphasizing that it was "just suspected." I added that if caught early, it was very curable, and that it seemed mine was an early diagnosis. I emphasized that it might be a misdiagnosis, anyway. If so, Dr. Schwartz would close me up and not do the operation. Philippa was sympathetic and concerned but her hands were full, something I knew well. But when Anastasia offered to come over and look after me for the week after surgery, I jumped at the offer.

Those calls made, I breathed a sigh of relief and drove up to Connecticut. My house there had never been finished; my heart was engaged in the project only at the beginning. Now the place overwhelmed me. It felt like another mistake, its emptiness and size echoing loneliness, this time in soft, Swedish pastels.

I straightened up the house and then quickly made my way over to John's place, a late-eighteenth century farmhouse. Full of comfortable furniture and other objects, many of them put there by me, it had once been my home. I felt a stab of nostalgia. Comforted by seeing John and having his company, I reviewed what I had been doing, all the calls and appointments. He got on my case for wanting to seek so many other opinions and ask so many questions. He saw all that as an unnecessary toll on my energy, and didn't understand why it was important, as I had an excellent doctor. I explained that when I was satisfied that I knew enough, I would let go and surrender. Even though he didn't agree, he acquiesced. We went out for a really nice dinner in Kent, the neighboring town.

The next day I went back to the city. On that Monday, I got in to see Dr. Postley. It was the best thing that could have happened. Facing him at his desk, papers piled high, his wise face peering over his ubiquitous bow tie, we talked over everything. He got Nadine to call the sonogram specialist for that second opinion, and I left uplifted. He seemed very happy with the choice of Dr. Schwartz and the plan to recover in Connecticut. On Tuesday, Gloria, my 21st-century equivalent of the family's Louise and Lena, came in. Calm by nature and religious, she is a strong woman who had come to the United States from Honduras and survived many challenges. As she listened to my news, she responded that she had felt I had been "running on empty" (her words) recently and that she had been worried. She was visibly distressed. From then on, each Tuesday she produced plentiful, nourishing food from the galley kitchen—hearty meals of steaming brown rice or a smooth, organic soup created from Japanese kabocha pumpkin. Her mission was to look after me and to build me up pre-surgery. She seemed to have personal knowledge that I would be all right. "Mrs. Horn, you are a strong woman," she said more than once. I had no doubt that her God, at her request, was now positioned close by.

Gloria's response echoed an outpouring of concern from many friends. We don't always get to discover how people really feel. Now, all the positive and loving thoughts coming my way, sometimes from surprising corners, bolstered my spirits.

Not forgetting about other second opinions, I telephoned a former romance whose connections in the medical world included cutting-edge doctors. He gave me the number of a Dr. Schiff, then the chief of Obstetrics and Gynecology Services at Massachusetts General. An hour later, he rang back to say Dr. Schiff was waiting for my call. Before we hung up, he said that he felt my illness had to do with difficulties surrounding loving, allowing that it is hard to do loving right. As I didn't want to get into that kind of conversation, I thanked him for his help, silently acknowledging that he had picked up on something else I needed to think about when I had more time.

When I reached Dr. Schiff's department, he came right to the telephone. "Suspected ovarian cancer," I said when he asked about the diagnosis, and described the treatment recommended. His next question threw me. "Do you like sex?" I said I did. "Well, it might change after a hysterectomy. This operation changes things," he commented, suggesting that the surgery was a kind of total castration. When I asked him about hormones, he admitted he was adamantly opposed to hormone replacement. As the conversation wound down, he asked, almost as an afterthought, "Who is your doctor at Yale?" When I told him, I could picture the smile curving his lips. "Do whatever he says. He is one of the finest doctors in the world and you are very lucky to have him." My sleuthing was paying off. In select circles, I was learning, Dr. Schwartz walked on water.

The discovery process was giving me assurance. Necessary pieces seemed to be falling into place, eliminating gaps in my confidence. But I wasn't quite ready to stop. I wanted the second sonogram. A magician as always, Nadine called the research doctor, who had an excellent reputation as a diagnostician, getting me right in. I sat with him in his office after he looked at the cyst. He gave me the same answer: a suspect ovarian cyst with "dense material." Then, I broke into floods of wrenching tears, managing to halt the flow only when I saw how upset I was making him. It was comic, and I laughed through the tears. "It will be all right," he insisted. He was adamant, repeating *"You* will be all right," a remark I would hold on to and protect.

The day of my appointment at Memorial Sloan-Kettering arrived. I walked the few blocks to the hospital and sat down in a spiffy waiting room filled with blonde wood paneling and furniture, up-to-date magazines, and flourishing plants. Dr. Marx had arranged for me to see a Dr. Barakat, who specialized in "my" kind of cancer. Both punctual and matter-of-fact, Dr. Barakat allowed that the plan Yale had suggested was one possible approach. But he also suggested something entirely different: laparoscopic surgery to remove the offending ovary.

A procedure using laparoscopy would enter the uterus with tiny cameras and instruments, requiring less anesthetic than conventional surgery. Because it was easier on the body than full abdominal surgery, it promised a faster recovery and less time in the hospital. Dr. Barakat explained that after he removed the offending ovary, we would wait for the pathology results to come back before determining a plan for further treatment.

This idea was a complete shock. I had been expecting corroboration, never dreaming I'd get an entirely different opinion. A brand new option raised totally unexpected questions. Now I needed to find out about laparoscopic surgery. It felt daunting and confusing, another twist in the road.

Though Dr. Barakat had clearly been expert, there had been something uncomfortable about Memorial Sloan-Kettering. My meeting had seemed a little *too* businesslike, something I had never felt with Dr. Schwartz. The whole issue of my reproductive system also troubled me. I had accepted the idea of having my uterus and ovaries removed. The constant checking on the cyst was time consuming and worrisome and after the conversation with Dr. Schiff, I was reconsidering the hormones. Prempro was no longer the trendy gold standard, but had become controversial. Also, the reality of losing an organ began to register, as did the thought of not enjoying sex again. I wondered if it might not be possible to leave the healthy ovary in place.

I was going into the second week post-diagnosis. Although I'd learned a tremendous amount, time was closing in on me. I still felt as though I was oscillating up and down, like a yo-yo. I had to ask Dr. Schwartz about laparoscopic surgery, straightaway: why he didn't do it, and whether retaining one ovary was an option.

Waiting for my visit to Yale the following week, I was chewing my knuckles with apprehension. There were stories of doctors throwing fits when asked about an additional opinion. Although I didn't expect this of Dr. Schwartz, I also knew he was a man of strong beliefs. I hoped neither he nor I would become too upset when we spoke, and I prayed I'd know how to choose between the opposing courses.

Thoughts of becoming a burden preyed on me. I didn't want my children to have to look after me as my mother had done with Grandma Jeanne. There was also the disturbing possibility that my cancer would be hereditary. That would be too much to bear—to be carrying a deadly gene or mutation that might affect not only my daughters but my grand-daughter, even my nieces and their offspring. Later, the genetic counselor at Yale, Rachel Barnett, would tell me that my case doesn't fit the average picture of a hereditary carrier, but, for now, that worry was adding to the pile of woes.

I went back to Yale, officially for some blood work. I can't remember if I actually had an appointment with Dr. Schwartz but I just stalked him, waiting patiently as he finished rounds. I snared him at the end of a conversation in a corridor outside the cafeteria. When I had a chance to ask for a chat, he guided me to a small conference room and asked what was on my mind, smiling as always but clearly busy. As I braced myself to begin my questions, I remembered something he had said in our last appointment. "Don't ask me any question if you are not prepared for a truthful answer. I will always give the truth as I see it."

Somewhat sheepishly, I asked him about laparoscopic surgery, admitting I had made a visit to Memorial Sloan-Kettering. He was quite definite. "I am sure that somewhere in the world, there is a place for laparoscopic surgery," he said, "but not in my practice. I need to get inside, and with that kind of surgery I cannot get a good enough look." (I should note here that in a recent conversation with Dr. Schwartz, he informed me that he does accept and perform this type of surgery in certain instances.) He went on to explain that in Memorial Sloan-Kettering's plan, the surgeon would "hood" the ovary before removing it. Despite that, malignant cells could still spill out into the abdomen. "I don't think you would want that to happen," he said. No, I certainly didn't. The explanation had hit a bull's-eye. I was convinced: no laparoscopic surgery.

When I asked quickly about keeping the second ovary, he said no to that, too. "The ovaries tend to mimic each other. If it's cancer, I insist on taking them both." From that moment, the first phase of my journey was over. My friends and family were relieved when I let them know that I had placed myself under a cease-and-desist order and would do no more information gathering. I had my answers; I was ready to proceed forward.

Mustering inner strength and staying positive, I believe, has a profound bearing on the outcome. I was proud I hadn't let myself get pushed around, had stuck to my guns in getting information, and had given in on my terms when I was ready, but not a second before. Many hospitals have signature protocols for illnesses, and, in some cases, targeted cancer therapies. Given differences of opinion and the rapidity of change in today's world, it's important to know who does what and all about your options. There are enough uncertainties inherent in cancer and the process of going through it, without adding any doubts about whether or not you've made the best choice of treatment.

Though my course was settled for now, I hadn't abandoned my

proactive approach to this illness. From the beginning, Dr. Schwartz's words and manner had indicated urgency. He wanted me in the hospital quickly, which precluded complimentary or alternative medicine therapies although I briefly considered other approaches. While I knew that many people had been successful with alternative or complementary treatment, I believed this phase needed speedy attention, as Dr. Schwartz had called it "an aggressive cancer." I also knew that later, I would find the way to address my whole self rather than just my disease.

7

Tomorrow Takes Wing

Double, double, toil and trouble. Fire burn and
cauldron bubble.

—WILLIAM SHAKESPEARE

Decisions made, I let go a little, focusing on preparation for surgery. The fun part included a big shopping spree at Morning Sun, the local health food emporium. I left with my shopping bags bulging with food, all organic, in joyful anticipation of Anastasia's visit.

As I got the necessary hospital and insurance permissions, the time bled from one day into the next. Questions would crop up and I'd get a call, needing to find the answer to some bit of information I'd left off a form, or else something new and unexpected would be required. Most of my dealings at this point were by telephone, often with administrative people at Yale. I learned fast that whenever I spoke with someone, I needed to listen as best as I could. Anxiety tended to cause bits of essential information to slip through the cracks. Sometimes the discussion was too technical and difficult. Occasionally, I had to ask the same question over and over again. Sometimes I was tired or hesitant. But if I didn't persist in finding the answer, who would?

The phone work on insurance was a mixed bag at best. People on the other end of a line were sometimes unwilling to think out of the box or deliver anything but rote answers. Some held back, giving insufficient or inaccurate information. Others were very helpful, sharing tips about how best to negotiate the labyrinth. At times I gave up out of frustration, angry at the system. Just dealing with the telephone shattered any residual notions I had of being in control. "Days are where we live," said Phillip Larkin. Taking life day by day was what I was trying to do.

One of John's favorite maxims was that, "You get more flies with honey than vinegar." I played games on the telephone, finding it possible to make inroads, even progress, by emphasizing our collective humanity, so to speak. My challenge was to get people to be nice, to try and think—if not out of the box, just think! I slowed down, used charm, and even seductiveness. I would ask about the family, which seemed to work; there is the Samaritan in all of us.

As the surgery neared, I met with the nurses, Karen and Lisa, for further explanations of the surgery. They discussed what discomfort I might feel, what anesthetic they would use, what toxins any of the drugs might contain, what program they had in mind afterwards. These talks tended to have an oddly impersonal tone but they helped. The nurses were great. A hospital, especially a big hospital, is both a community and a corporate culture. The personal and emotional sides tend to be kept under wraps, although I hear that there is more counseling available now than when I was being treated.

Had I truly understood how nervous I was, I would have had a friend accompany me to take notes in these meetings. I would also have had units of blood taken and stored in case I needed a transfusion; requested copies of all my x-rays; and kept a more centralized record of doctors and materials sent from one place to another, especially as I was creating a document library. But as is so often said, hindsight is twenty-twenty. Today, I use my blog and speaking to suggest strategies, including these, that will help other women navigate this difficult labyrinth of insurance permissions, hospitals and all the other, as yet, unknowns.

It was now late May. I had a June date for surgery but was worried that the tumor might be growing too fast, that I might be running out of time. All the precious time I felt I'd lost or wasted in life gnawed at me. But I also knew I was too hard on myself. That had to change. I had to think only of the next step and stop obsessing about either the past or the future. For now, the present was what was important. "Just put one foot in front of the other," John gently suggested. So that's what I did.

I had another chiropractic session with Nancy and felt good after getting tweaked and straightened out. She believed I was somehow amazing and respected all the work I'd done to figure out my life—the perpetual quest for improvement. There was yet another stalwart who was sure I'd be okay. All this trust helped me find courage when it flagged and to be strong when I despaired.

Preparing for this surgery was something like preparing for a singing performance: lots of physical work to do, without much time to do it in. The comparison helped, because a disciplined regime kicked in. I did chiropractic, acupuncture, walking, exercise, Alexander Technique, and weekly massage. I also ate far better than I had been–for starters, dropping the Doritos. I ate healthy, non-processed foods, strong in fiber. I also loaded up on animal protein like fish and chicken, because protein is the food for cellular regeneration. Soothing foods like brown rice and miso support the immune system and are supposed to promote healing, so they were included as well. Mine was a busy kitchen at that time. Just as well, because I was pretty sure the food in the hospital would be awful.

Good breathing and meditation helps singers withstand the rigors of performance and manage nerves. I decided I would do those, too. Finally, "divas" drink water religiously to flush out toxins, so I followed suit. I have no doubt that this healthy behavior helped me deal with surgery and its physical aftermath quicker and better than it would have, had I not taken those steps. But the mental attitude was just as valuable. My preparation was put into a proactive, powerful context, and reminded me that I was a person with gifts and capacities, not just illnesses or flaws.

Jan Troy, an Iyengar yoga teacher practicing nearby in Cornwall,

CT, was a great support during this time. Jan had beaten a serious health problem with a dedicated yoga practice. She's a soul mate; we call each other "goddess," shouting it into the telephone when we speak. "Hey, goddess, how are you?" we scream. Iyengar yoga focuses on alignment. The breathing associated with the postures, an exercise in itself, reduces stress levels and is thought to release toxins. My yoga practice had been spasmodic, but now I returned to class to strengthen my back, leg and shoulder muscles, as well as to work on breathing and relaxation. I'd been told I would be lying down for five days after my surgery. A stretched and limber body would hopefully combat stiffness and weakness.

Friends helped out from near and far. Two special women originally from the Midwest, my brother's long-term lady friend, Miles Dumont, and my singing teacher, Marianne Challis, gave me support so warm it verged on mothering. They seemed to have all the time in the world when I called, no matter how needy. I hold that west of Pennsylvania something happens to the female DNA that gives rock-solid grounding. It must be the water.

Even people I hardly knew were generous and kind. One friend knew that Jane Whitney, the former talk show hostess and writer, had been a patient of Dr. Schwartz. I knew Jane's husband, Lindsay, so I picked up the phone and called her. She gave glowing reports about Dr. Schwartz, who had treated her for what was apparently a very complicated case. As a journalist would, she gave me a full rundown. I appreciated her willingness to share her personal experiences with this disease, although I could also understand why others preferred to stay silent.

I found I needed both solitude and company during this period. Each day, I spent some time staying quiet, without TV or telephone or any other distractions. I wanted to feel some deeper connection to myself, go more deeply inside to see if I could to find some respite from worry. I'd been taught Transcendental Meditation several years before, and started meditating regularly again, after a long hiatus. I also used a former Alexander Technique teacher's method of getting more grounded and connected. That had always been a challenge for me, as it is for many abuse survivors; our tendency can be to live as observers of our own lives, keeping experiences almost out of body. My teacher would tell me to "try to find that little speck of consciousness inside yourself," pointing to an area underneath my breastbone. That tiny speck is wily and elusive but it, or something like it, exists and a special quietness and connection can happen when it's found through concentration. The practice seemed to help me stay grounded, even if it was only the trying that mattered.

It was essential to make sure that all hospital stays, medication, surgery, and any other services to be covered by the HMO were in place. I nervously made sure again and again the insurance was taken care of. Scared by the thought of some horrendous bill, I didn't trust others to get it right. In the end there was only one glitch, which Yale fixed for me. God bless these selfless secretary/assistants who know how to negotiate the health system—in this case, the amazing Betsy Baird.

I bought Bernie Siegel's *Life, Love and Miracles*, a classic that's still in print. It kept me in stitches, no pun intended. Humor distracts, and may even increase the body's immune cells. This book was as good for me as reading *Auntie Mame* the first time. I walked in a local nature preserve, enjoying the warm, gentle weather. I visited Dr. Nancy yet again, getting an exercise to strengthen my adrenal glands.

Despite all of this, sometimes I felt as if I had four flat tires. The old demons of uncertainty and fear wore me down at times. I'd give myself a pep talk to pull myself around the next corner. My mind was constantly chattering away. "Did I remember to make that call?" or "Where's that pink nightgown I like?" Sometimes I felt terribly sad, my thoughts hammering away about losses suffered and potential unmet. Guilt and sadness are a horrible combination, especially when their raw edges conjoin. I tried to tell myself that this wasn't the right time for the grand puzzle of life to be sorted out.

When I was in that place of sorrow, everything seemed a little unfair. Yet I also knew I had much for which to be grateful. No one depended on me for meals, house cleaning or support during this three-week window. I thanked my lucky stars, whichever ones they were, for that freedom, as well as for all of my other blessings.

In *About Alice*, Calvin Trillin wrote that cancer can cause a loss of identity to those going through it. But cancer didn't rob me of my identity. Instead, it was already helping me find a new one. I had spent years meandering. With my diagnosis, I knew that part of my life was over. I was facing something very serious—out of the ordinary, but not final. I was doing all I could to be the very best patient I could be, with a co-operative body and a collaborative rather than resistant attitude. I had gone into training, and felt as well prepared as I could be. I could be scared at times, but I knew I had a good chance to win the fight.

The brain can release chemicals to sedate and calm. In the remaining three days before my surgery, I had entered a new space, moving past frenzy and towards acceptance. I was well and truly ready for part two of my journey.

8

The Tsunami

What is to give light must endure burning.

— VIKTOR FRANKL

Everything had been done, checked, rechecked and checked again. The insurance, the trip to the hospital, the caregiver I would need after surgery, all had been arranged. A few days before going to New Haven, I had a more frivolous thought. If I did die on the operating table, I didn't want some funeral parlor to mess me up. I went to the hairdresser and had a full set of highlights, the works, spending $250 plus a big tip. It was worth every penny. I didn't want to be remembered as a woman with bad hair or as a lousy tipper.

Three nights before D-Day, I started packing. My reputation in that department is notorious. This time, I only wanted to take what I needed, not the kitchen sink, as was my usual pattern. Nonetheless, I did end up with an extra bag on top of the usual three but they were all very small. I packed all of the magazines I hadn't read and several books, including some mysteries and inspirationals. My make-up was packed, plus two nice nighties for when the surgical gown was dispatched and a short flannelette robe with little roses, fine as a cover-up for visitors. Slippers, a hairbrush, a toiletries bag with nice soap, and of course, my Filofax completed this dazzling collection of stuff. I knew John would roll his eyes at all this, and be thankful we weren't married any more. (A trip to an airport in Sicily with no porter seemed stuck in his brain forever.)

I got to bed early but I didn't sleep well, feeling strangely elated but also calm at the same time. I think that must have been because the first part of this ordeal and journey would be over soon. The immediate problem was being dealt with in a way I sanctioned and had decided on for myself.

John had offered to drive me to New Haven on the day of the surgery. We left his apartment around six a.m., the morning sky a milky, indecisive grey, no sun and no clouds. We headed over to the west side of the city and picked up Marion Bedrick, an old friend who'd offered to stay in the hospital until I was back in my room. Briefly, I attempted my own brand of class-clown humor, trying to act like this wasn't a big deal. By the time we had driven up the Merritt Parkway to Greenwich or thereabouts, the radio was making the only sounds.

At the hospital, we checked in with no glitches. I was apprehensive, but didn't want to show it. I dropped my things in the appointed locker room, a grim little chamber. Next, I was led into a curtained cubicle, from where I said goodbye to both John and Marion. She went to a waiting room; he drove back to New York. The curtain suddenly screeched down a metal rod; I felt this was the moment of being cut off from the outside world. Changing slowly into the hospital's simple blue gown, I dug into my purse and gave the new blonde streaks a quick, final brush.

A handsome young doctor appeared, introducing himself as one of Dr. Schwartz's team. He asked me to get on the gurney so he could escort me to the operating room. I always liked talking to attractive men—even, I joked silently to myself, if they were about to remove an organ. But I felt my throat clutch a little. With a forced smile, I hopped on the gurney for a very solitary ride. I can't really describe what that was like except to say it was a unique experience, knowing it was a voyage into unknown territory.

Somewhere on the way, I was shaved. I remember little about it except that I closed my eyes during the process and then looked down and saw that I was bare, completely bare. I also remember that it was a nurse and not the young doctor who did the procedure. Next, I was wheeled towards the operating room, then parked on the side. There I met Dr. Sinatra, the anesthetist. Unable to resist the obvious question, he said he was not related but he would be glad to sing something anyway. From then on, I felt okay. He had a lovely smile and a twinkle in his eye—comforting at a time when I was scared silly. I smiled as he gave me the first anesthetic, which would sedate me before the big one to put me out. As I was wheeled into the operating room, thinking I was wide awake but relaxed, I requested that no one swear or say negative things, since I had read that patients may hear what is said, even when sedated. Chatting away about the romance between two of the residents and counting to ten, I heard Dr. Schwartz's calm voice and some laughter in the background.

The next thing I knew, I was awake and in the recovery room. My eyes told me I had cancer: looking at the big round clock, I could see that I'd been in surgery for over five hours. Even semi-conscious, I figured this was no little exploratory operation, but rather the real McCoy. Naked except for the blue gown and hospital bracelet, exhausted and groggy, I was relieved I'd made it through and not yet focused on what they might have found.

At three in the afternoon or so, I was wheeled into my room, falling asleep again. When I awoke, several pretty bouquets of flowers were waiting for me. Marion was patiently sitting by my bed, a welcome sight. She told me that Dr. Schwartz had come out of the operating room several times to report on his progress. In one of those moments, he had asked her if he could remove my cervix. Apparently some complication was compromising our earlier decision to keep it. Amazed at the request, she told me she had declined. That exchange seemed rather strange to me. Technically, I had received what's called a supracervical hysterectomy, a little less than a total removal of everything. I was happy she saved any body parts that didn't have to go.

Marion added, "Dr. Schwartz came in after you were back in the room and told you he had found cancer in your ovary. I was amazed that you were so stoic. I would have jumped out the window." I had no memory of that conversation. I could, and did, mask my true feelings much more back then than I do now. Probably I was just groggy. Certainly, I had suspected there might be cancer when receiving the original diagnosis three weeks before, so maybe the news just wasn't a huge surprise.

Marion had been sitting in the hospital all day. I thanked her and we said goodbye so she could go back to New York in daylight. After she left I dozed on and off, still under the influence of the anesthetic, oblivious to the hard pillows and the paraphernalia for draining the incision. There was no pain, just discomfort from the drains and the hard bed. It was unfamiliar and noisy, with the plastic under sheet crunching as I moved, nothing like my lovely bed with the crisp white sheets at home. However, I was pretty wiped out, so I figured I wouldn't mind, especially after the drains were removed.

I awoke again around six p.m. to see the beautiful, loving face of Marianne Challis standing over my bed. Singing teacher to the stars as well as to me, she was holding a book and a brown paper bag that concealed a quart of peach ice cream. She had done her regular commute from New York to Fairfield, Connecticut, then hit Baskin-Robbins and driven to Yale, hoping the ice cream wouldn't melt while she waited for me to wake up. As I looked into her soulful eyes, I broke down and sobbed, "I have ovarian cancer." Her face melted with empathy. That and her Midwestern solidity—qualities greater than gold—imbued me with strength.

Marianne handed over the large pink book she was holding in the other hand, saying that while she knew it wasn't what I usually read, I might dip into it here and there. Over the summer I did, finding the positive aphorisms designed to give just a little boost without too much thinking. I don't remember the title, only that it shared the kind of wisdom associated with grandmothers, lemonade, and common sense.

It was a good visit for me. After Marianne left, I dug into the ice cream. It occurred to me that I didn't really know that much about ovarian cancer despite my investigations. I worried that the cancer might be more advanced than they had suggested. But no one knew about that, until the results came back from Pathology. For the moment, my long-term outlook was limited to the next ten minutes. I figured out how to use the TV remote and sort out all the wires around my bed. Next job was to maneuver the rolling IV stand and myself into the bathroom. Those first steps took considerable effort, and I was decidedly uncomfortable. The incision had cut vertically through abdominal muscle, causing severe trauma there and around my pelvic area. It would leave those areas weak for a long time.

Successfully back in bed, I sat looking into space, the rolling tray over my knees. There was a telephone to deal with along with the tubes and other paraphernalia. John called, and so did the girls. All three had sent flowers which were waiting for me. I told them all how beautiful they were and how nice it was to speak to them. To the girls, I explained that I was doing fine, that Marion and Marianne had visited, and that according to the doctor I'd come through very well. Saying that I loved them, I added that I would speak to Philippa soon and see Anastasia in four or five days. At some point a dinner tray appeared, holding what reminded me of the food I had seen in movies about prisons: a scoop of reconstituted mashed potatoes separated from a couple of slices of dry chicken drenched in a brown gravy, accompanied by a yogurt and some white bread. None of it was appetizing, though I hear the hospital's food has improved since then. Nothing could have been more different from the flavorful, healthy food I had been eating in the run-up to the surgery. But the creamy peach ice cream had hit the spot, so this sad meal didn't matter so much.

If I'd had any doubts that I didn't want to be in the hospital for one minute longer than necessary, looking at that tray ended them. I scarfed down more spoonfuls of Marianne's softening ice cream, making another considerable dent. Singers are supposed to stay away from dairy products, which supposedly cause mucus. But right then I was a patient, not a singer, and I didn't want it to melt. I remember making a mental note to drink lots of fluids, especially water, which would help flush the anesthetic toxins out of my body. I would also avoid the sugary fruit juices that seemed to be standard hospital fare.

At night the ward staffing was efficient, but more skeletal and mostly part-time. I never saw the same night person twice. Most of them were not full-fledged nurses, but nursing assistants. They were efficient but didn't always have time to offer more than the basics: checking my temperature, asking if I'd had a bowel movement, helping with problems of sleep or pain by handing out pills.

I woke up several times during that first night and every other night I spent in the hospital. As I did so, I felt a deep loneliness and sense of strangeness. Lying in semi-darkness, I knew I was surrounded by other women in distress, each like me, in her own little cell and struggling with the implications of her particular illness. That first night reminded me of Ingmar Bergman's *The Hour of the Wolf*, a film about that time of deep night when people either die or are born. In those moments, I understood isolation and loneliness in a new way.

One morning at around three a.m., I awoke from a half-sleep to find a woman with curved and iridescent fingernails more than three inches long adjusting my bed covers and fiddling with a bed pan. As I jumped, I thought this was Walt Disney at his wildest. The amount of bacteria harbored underneath those things could start a pandemic. It was a comic experience, yet also scary. If I ever commanded a floor of nurses, those nails would be banned.

The nurses made it very clear that I should get up and walk as soon as possible, uncomfortable though it might be. They explained that walking would help to stabilize and strengthen the body. I was to be mindful of stepping carefully to avoid a fall. I made little walking tours around my floor of the hospital, feeling more and more comfortable with my sidekick IV frame. By now I could syncopate our movements; I was Fred, it was Ginger.

By Saturday morning, two days after the surgery, the effects of the anesthetic had fully worn off. My head felt clearer and my body and abdomen felt better, too, all things considered. I had had some sleep and cleaned myself up. The fabulous hair streaks were holding nicely and the nightgown and robe I had chosen made me feel reasonably presentable. In bed and feeling virtuous after a walk, I was surprised to see Dr. Schwartz come in after a knock. He looked natty in a blue blazer, gray slacks and loafers—very different from the man in the blue scrubs I had seen two mornings before. Seeing a wonderful warm smile on his face, I reached out and give him a hug of gratitude. He returned it, his face reflecting both surprise and kindness.

He seemed optimistic, based on what he had seen during the surgery. His visit seemed more like a pleasant, routine drop-in to see a patient than an ominous conference telling me to prepare my will and talk to my family. He told me he had given me a "nice scar," an oxymoron meaning a "bikini scar." I wasn't sure if he had received the final pathology report regarding the section taken while I was on the table. That would tell us if there was cancer remaining in my body, but I was too scared to ask him. If he mentioned chemotherapy that day, I didn't hear it.

The only thing I remember clearly from that conversation is requesting (in fact, demanding) hormones, even though estrogen replacement therapy was increasingly frowned on by that time. But I was determined, having lost both ovaries suddenly, not to be catapulted into instant menopause on top of everything else. Later I discovered that estrogen loss or reduction can create lots of other problems as well. To my surprise, Dr. Schwartz agreed without hesitation, saying he would tell one of the residents to supply me. (He would not have allowed it if my cancer had been estrogen-driven.) He recommended intra-vaginal estrogen, a medication called Vagifem that was preferred by his department at Yale.

On Monday morning, the same handsome young resident I had seen on the first day came in for a visit. Full of good humor, he asked how it was going for me. I found him very cute; since I could still respond to an attractive fellow, I thought, maybe I hadn't been thrown into menopause after all. Nevertheless, I wanted those hormones. Recalling that 90s bumper sticker, "I'm out of estrogen and I've got a gun," I wondered if I had a Ma Barker rampage in me. The resident was surprised that Dr. Schwartz was prescribing the Vagifem. I had the sense that he really didn't know that much about which cancers were "no-no's" when it came to hormone replacement or that hormones were not much discussed with the residents. Anyway, I didn't care; I just wanted them. He said he would check with Dr. Schwartz and send them around to me.

Once the polite banter and estrogen conversation was finished, the resident launched into a description of my chemotherapy. I was shocked, as this discussion came straight out of the blue. The type of carcinoma I had, said he, was an aggressive cancer; although mine was Stage One, chemotherapy was Dr. Schwartz's standard approach. From what I could gather, his reasoning was that even though tests might indicate that a patient was clear after surgery, dormant cancer or cells too small to see under the microscope might still be present. After he left, I had a mini meltdown. It was totally unexpected and very distressing. I had no recollection of any previous discussion about chemotherapy.

Over my five days in the hospital, I developed my own little routine of walking, reading, eating, TV, talking on the telephone, seeing a few visitors and dozing. It was tolerable enough, especially as my stay was finite and short. I was touched by the attention, especially the flowers. Constant drop-ins from both administration and medical staff also kept me busy, some wanting to know about my insurance, others telling me how to sign up for the chemo. One asked if I would like some foot reflexology, which I found relaxing. Yale seemed ahead of the curve on many of these alternative practices, using acupuncture and studying aspects of traditional Chinese medicine. No one said anything further about my status or how serious my cancer was.

By departure day, I was more than ready to leave. Anastasia and John drove together from New York together to collect me, with the plan that he would drop Annie and me to the house in Bethlehem. On that day, no obstacles stood in the way of my discharge from the hospital, although I was still tired and weak. I packed up, brushed the highlights, put on some make-up, and gave the remaining flowers to the people on the floor. By the time Annie and John arrived, I had been packed and ready for over an hour, diplomatically refusing lunch.

I was so excited to see them both. Sitting in my first and only wheelchair to date, they wheeled me to the elevator, Anastasia at the helm. Waiting for the elevator, I suddenly dissolved into floods of tears. Though I was acutely aware that the outcome could have been very different, I was leaving with my life and some hope, each a cause for celebration. Bad news, yes, that the ovarian cyst had been malignant. But at least for now I had a future, an enormous relief for one who had unfinished business in her life. Weak as I was, I was determined to survive, regain my physical strength, and confront those loose ends of mine which needed tying up.

The drive to my house in Bethlehem passed quickly. As John's car approached the proud yellow house perched on the crest of a small hill, its driveway chronically rutted by strong rainfall, the sun hit my eyes. There was still precious little landscaping, as I had been unsure of how to proceed and had largely lost interest. But everything looked pretty, bathed in its late spring warmth, and the light flooded the windows of the colonial-style house as we drove up to the side doors. The front door was never used except by the Seventh Day Adventists when they came to call, mostly when I was in the tub or taking a nap.

The house felt strange and unlived-in, with an aura of stillness and stasis throughout. Time had halted in it while I was gone, and the air was slightly stale. John did not tarry after helping with the bags. Normally I would have rushed around, obsessively adjusting a chair position, cleaning a sink, or trying to find some flowers. Now I just wanted to rest and spend time with my daughter. She had traveled a long way to help me. I was grateful, though it felt odd that that the shoe was on the other foot, the child caring for the mother rather than the other way around.

We organized ourselves quickly. Annie was soon on my case about not drinking enough water, appearing at my bedside with a determined Nurse Ratched look, proffering large glasses of H_2O, and explaining why they were necessary. Delighted I had such a sensible daughter in charge, I tried to obey. I've tried to follow this advice—her mantra, ever since—though not always successfully.

Both my daughters are fabulous cooks. Anastasia produced endless nourishing meals during her stay. When one of her old friends from Wesleyan College came to visit for a day or two, it felt like old times, with family entering my life again. By the time she and Meredith had to leave, the house was full of flowers.

Anastasia had to return to England—her visit had already taken up more time than she could spare from her job in London. Meredith left for the airport with her. They took a car provided by a local service. Evidently they spent the entire trip giggling. The elderly driver kept saying that Anastasia's face, fair-haired and blue-eyed, reminded him of Ella Fitzgerald, which both girls found hysterical. It had meant everything to have her there with me; I would miss her.

They left late in the afternoon, the sun was slowly sinking. It was the first time I had been totally alone since surgery, and that feeling of aloneness lasted for a long time.

9

Chemotherapy

Don't tread on me.

— General Christopher Gadsden

From before the surgery I knew I would need help for some time afterward. Dr. Schwartz had said that if possible, I should go up and down stairs only once a day for the first few weeks. I was also told I couldn't drive a car for six weeks, a standard restriction after abdominal surgery. My friends, the Kinsolvings, had recommended Dale Mc-Braerity as a caregiver. Dale is an imposing presence: tall, with longish blonde hair and good nails (mine are lousy, so I always notice). She is direct, endowed with a definite no-nonsense attitude, and she doesn't miss much. I have no doubt in another incarnation she was a great warrior, a Saladin perhaps, fighting for her causes. Yet she's also a true angel: warm, compassionate, smart as a whip and a lot of fun.

Dale knew how to do it all, offering sensible approaches and lots of ideas, including a list of requisite post-surgery items. The first thing she suggested buying was a bench for the shower, which would provide extra height (and therefore stability), also keeping the scars dry. Next, she wanted an elevated toilet seat, again for stability and to make it easier for me to raise myself up when I was on my own. In the beginning she came a few days a week, sometimes twice a day, to help me bathe, make food, and just talk. Since she became my savior, I felt fortunate that she lived about only twenty-five minutes from me.

I didn't realize it then, but because of chemo, our relationship would extend all through the summer months. I grew to love and depend on her, especially during my roughest emotionally charged moments. Dale gives her full, undistracted attention and focus; it became obvious she was gifted. Even when she wasn't working for me anymore, she would on occasion call and say she'd like to drop over. This wonderful woman was always hopeful, even when we had our conversations about dying and death. I met and liked her husband, John, as well. When she would pop in to say hello, glowing and excited, her nails or hair just done because they were doing something special that night, it was evident that they had sustained the romance in their long marriage. That was a gentle reminder of what was lacking in my life, but also of what I aspired to.

Dale thought I should have a view and be near the kitchen, so I moved downstairs during the day. A friend had a spare bed, which was moved in and placed by the living room's front window. The vista looked down my tree-lined driveway and out to the main road, a quiet country lane with hardly any traffic. As I recovered from each round of chemo, I passed many hours gazing soulfully out that window, usually not thinking about much at all, an herbal tea at my side. I was smart enough to resist "Type A" behavior and avoided trying to do it all faster, better and brighter than anyone else. Anyway, I didn't have the strength for it. Each day, in the afternoon, I walked outside alone or with Dale, challenging myself to do a little more every time, my reward being one of her grilled cheese and ham sandwiches. Not rushing was kind of a new sensation for me, as was walking very slowly. I felt some frustration, but then found myself liking the pace.

Given the ban on driving, I had to find drivers to take me anywhere, but especially to and from New Haven, not only for the chemo sessions but to do the important blood work before each treatment. The lab work determined if I had enough white cells to proceed. If I didn't, the next round of chemo had to be postponed. Such delays were tricky. If too much time passed between treatments, I learned, the chemo would be much less effective. John, William and other friends pitched in to help with the many trips, which sometimes ended with fun overnights and pampering.

In the meantime, there was a celebration in the works. My 60th birthday was approaching. I felt no need to make plans, but Dale insisted on throwing a luncheon party at her house. This would be the first birthday party that someone else had planned and thrown for me in a very long time. My expensive highlights, though guaranteed to fall out, were holding nicely. I got all dressed up for the first time since the diagnosis. Guests included John, the Kinsolvings, Marianne Challis and her husband Frank Root, as well as their young daughter and her friend. John picked me up, driving me to the super-special log cabin house owned by Dale and *her* John, a charming Irishman with a big smile and hearty laugh. Just as we were leaving my driveway, John looked over at me. "You are a lovely woman," he said, as if we had just met. If some of your female parts have been recently sliced out, however skillfully, that's a nice thing to hear. Looking in the back seat, I saw a big white paper box with simple string knotting the top. I knew my cake was inside, with a saucy Miss Piggy who would be revealed later on as the mascot on top.

The McBrearitys had created a festive party atmosphere, balloons and votive candles everywhere, champagne chilling in a bucket in the living room. The house was full of people I cared about; I could feel their affection radiating back at me. That and the fuss over my birthday almost overwhelmed me. Admiring, even a little envious, of the close relationships of the McBrearitys, the Kinsolvings, the Roots and their family, I felt cherished by everyone at that moment. The emotion sent shivers up my body. As the cake was brought in, a discreet six candles blazing, I savored the sheer outrageous willfulness of Miss Piggy. There she was, supreme on the top of the cake, helping me to blow out the candles: pearls, curls, fake eyelashes, other girly accoutrements and all. The singing and clapping almost overwhelmed me as I blew out my candles and made the obvious wish.

And so the summer of my chemotherapy commenced. I soon discovered that chemotherapy is something like marriage: you don't really know what it's like until you experience it. Some of the surprises were big, others small, but surprises there constantly were.

Yale had a chemotherapy room designated just for gynecological patients. It was small, even intimate, with comfortable leatherette reclining chairs in assorted colors for the three- to five-hour treatment sessions. Nurses Karen and Lisa were always around, diligently checking and clucking, their office adjacent to this room. I dealt most often with Karen Coombs, a capable, attractive blond who usually wore well-cut khaki pants and exuded efficiency, the sort of person you'd trust to get you out of a pickle. As I sat for the first time, needle-bound, I asked her whether I ever would get sick after the chemo sessions. Peering down at me over her horn rims, she said, "If you get sick, we haven't done our job." Thanks to IV medications given at the start of each treatment and little red tablets given afterward, I never did. I felt close to it a couple of times, but I never missed a meal!

In the chemo room, everyone's look grows similar. We all had pale facial skin and stoic expressions, and wigs or turbans covering our bald heads. Our routines were the same as well. We would each settle into a chaise, an outstretched arm or open shirt where the needle went in to receive our elixirs. Some women knitted, others watched TV. We were like a strange team, all trying for the same endgame: to reclaim our futures.

Of course, there were differences. Some of the women around me looked very ill, frail and tired, others surprisingly healthy and normal. (I found that beyond the paleness and other side effects, chemo does wonders for the skin.) One or two patients were ushered to a bed behind a curtain because they were too upset, sick or emotionally fragile to sit in the shared area. I remember a woman with Stage 3 ovarian cancer. Type A from the get-go, she made a point of announcing that she had driven herself over from Guilford, about 12 miles away. She planned to drive back and then go to work the next day. She seemed so wired up and determined not to rest that it concerned me. I wondered if she was always "on" in that way, deciding that wasn't a good thing to be in our circumstances.

Dr. Schwartz and the handsome young resident had told me about my treatment program, which included a drug cocktail of cisplatin and paclitaxel. Twelve years later, that combination still seems to be the preferred treatment. The paclitaxel, better known as Taxol, is a compound originally derived from the Pacific yew tree, though it's now synthetically produced. I was lucky to escape the infections it can produce thanks to the lower production of white blood cells it may cause, but I didn't escape the 100% guaranteed hair loss predicted by Nurse Karen.

She predicted it would begin exactly fourteen days after the first round of chemo, and she was right almost to the hour. On the fourteenth morning, as the sun woke me by streaming into my bedroom, I rolled over to find a clump of those expensive highlights lying on my pillow. At first, I thought the clump could be a mouse. A couple of weeks later, I went into the bathroom only to realize that my eyebrows and lashes were beginning to fall out, unevenly at first. Throughout the summer, I found clumps of hair here and there all over the house. Karen and her knowledge rose higher and higher in my estimation on each discovery.

Hair loss can sound like a minor thing given all of the other painful and dangerous challenges cancer patients face, especially since the hair usually grows back to look much like it did before the illness. Yet losing such a visible and symbolic marker of identity—one that is also often a source of pride—can give rise to powerful feelings. Jean Schleski, a therapist at the Rocky Mountain Cancer Centers in Denver, has written, "When survivors lose their pride, they also lose part of their identity." She describes a session in which one woman stated, "I've lost my hair, I've lost my breasts, I've gotten fat because of the chemo." I knew my femininity resided in a deeper place than my hair. But undoubtedly, people looked at and treated me differently, more as a cancer patient than as a woman. For a while, I felt unfeminine, as though the chemo had altered the woman I had been. The physical changes came as a psychological shock.

The hair loss, more than anything else, drove home the damage being inflicted to my body. If the drugs could affect the outside of me to that degree, what must be happening on the inside? It was obvious that any notion I had of being in control was definitely an illusion. That realization was humbling. Also, this was a highly visible sign that marked me out for people's sympathy; I was too proud to like being the target of pity, however well-meant. Finally, my hair loss raised my worry that I might have irretrievably lost my essential sexuality. That fear had been ongoing since the surgery, long before I started looking like a billiard ball.

A victim mentality sometimes struck, but I struggled not to let that kind of thinking take hold. When that little voice asked if I'd lost my sexuality, I tried answering, "What the hell, if you have, you have. Fight back. Make yourself up, wear blusher and lipstick, dress in something attractive—that always helps." But those were tough moments.

Dale and I found a couple of inexpensive and colorful velvet turbans and some wigs. They made me feel glamorous in a kind of 40s-cinema way and were easy to wear, but I still looked a little like a plucked chicken. Our forays around the state of Connecticut in search of headgear were our version of Thelma and Louise, thankfully with a less fatal outcome. Dale drives very fast; though I badly wanted the wigs, I also wanted to make sure we didn't have a car crash. I was already spending enough time in hospitals. Checking the speedometer—discreetly, I thought—one afternoon as we whizzed along Route 84, Dale finally asked if I thought she drove too fast. I must have been staring at the speedometer, knuckles white at my side, so I gulped and nodded. We both had a good laugh. After that, she let up on the accelerator for good.

We drove miles and miles, checking out any and every address in the Yellow Pages, until one day we edged into a little strip mall and hit pay dirt in Waterbury. That outing produced a set of false "bangs" I could tuck under the turbans, making them look more natural. We also left with two wigs. Both short, one was a blonde bobbed number and one was red. I had always wanted to experience being a redhead, and this seemed like the moment. But my treatments were in June,

July and August. The weather was hot, and so were the wigs. They didn't have much of an outing until the fall. The red wig soon landed on a closet shelf, my Rita Hayworth moment over, but the other made it through the autumn.

My best attempts to look presentable notwithstanding, my illness was evident. One afternoon, a K-Mart checkout lady saw my hairless face and turbaned head and said, "You've got cancer, don't you?"

"Yes, I do," I replied.

"What kind do you have?" she queried, looking at me sideways as she packaged my purchases.

"I have ovarian cancer," said I.

"Everyone dies from that, don't they?" this paragon of tact and diplomacy parried.

"I am hoping to be the first person who does not," I said grandly, trying to convince myself.

Inside, I tried to be charitable. Not everyone wants to be around a cancer patient, or any ill person for that matter: intimations of death or sickness inspire the fear of possibly being next. But as I left, I was pretty sure she was looking at me as someone K-Mart would certainly lose as a customer.

All these drugs have many other potential side effects, though not everyone experiences all of them. Almost no one escapes the fatigue and aching, especially after the second and third sessions. My side effects included numbness, officially known as peripheral neuropathy. Causing tingling in my arm, hand or legs, often in the middle of the night, the neuropathy made it difficult to fasten small buttons and manage other such tasks. In some instances, this can become permanent in extremities such as fingers and toes. But it can also come and go...or just go. In my case, after a while, it pretty much disappeared. Other nerve damage resulted in a mild form of fecal incontinence. A surgeon in New York said that the chemotherapy had probably damaged some rectal nerves. As a result, my brain and body no longer accurately sensed the residue left over after a bowel movement. The way to handle that, I found, was simply to remember that there might be more to come, and make sure it was all taken care of. The problem seems nicely under control now, but at the time it was just another of those unexpected surprises slightly battering away at my sense of self.

Cisplatin also works by interrupting cell division, preventing DNA production in the cancer cells so they can no longer reproduce. Although patients are tested beforehand with a urine collection to determine the proper dose, it can damage the kidneys, gut and blood as well as causing neuropathy. Its special feature is the loss of taste, though it seems to try to compensate for that by leaving a metallic taste of its own in the mouth. As a final memento of Cisplatin, my fingernails and toenails have acquired permanent deep vertical ridges that I have been told will never go away. They are permanent markers of the disease.

The monitoring of my white blood cell count continued throughout my rounds of chemo. When my white cell count dropped, I was given Neupogen (filgrastim) to increase the count. After the initial treatment with this drug, one night I woke up with a feeling like a radiator with an air block—or as though a small hammer was banging inside my leg. The pain was strong, but not unbearable. I knew it was my bones—I could locate and feel where it was coming from. Oddly, I found myself kind of fascinated by the symptom. The sensation diminished after the first and second rounds of chemo. Just when I got used to it, any fascination with the new gone, the doctors cut the drug, believing it problematic for me. I also felt as though my legs were being hammered when I walked. The nurses said they hadn't heard of reactions like that before.

The memory of my first shot of Neupogen is an oddly happy one. I was to be ensconced for a few nights with Susan and William Kinsolving, so Yale arranged for the shot to be delivered to their house. About five one afternoon, an attractive woman drove up while we were all in the kitchen, talking and laughing while planning dinner. It was the nurse, delivering a package with the doses. Having prepared us on what to do, she went off on her rounds in her little SUV. The Neupogen went in the fridge next to the red wine. William, my cabaret singing partner on several occasions, then revealed yet another facet of his amazing and wide-ranging abilities. One of their two gorgeous daughters, Eliza, had been diagnosed with juvenile diabetes years before, so he knew how to give injections. Just before dinner, he delivered the jab so painlessly, I was amazed. We then all had a glass of wine and a leisurely meal. Later, I ascended in my turban up to what was now being called "my room"—a room, they asserted, that would always be waiting for me.

With that drug, it wasn't always such smooth sailing. After my third course of Neupogen, my white cell count soared to over 80,000 (normal is 7,000 to 8,000) and then crashed. The next round of chemo had to be postponed. I was upset, and Karen, my capable nurse, was also shaken by the extraordinarily high numbers. Stupidly, as I put down the telephone after learning that next chemo session was off, I felt I had somehow failed.

The night I heard this, I was supposed to have dinner with my friend Hiram Williams. He had lost his former partner to cancer. When I called, in tears, to say that I just didn't feel up to going out, he explained to me that such a crash wasn't unusual. He was frustrated and annoyed that the doctors hadn't given me guidance on this part of the treatment. But of course, I was relieved to be reassured that the postponement wasn't unusual. It assuaged my fear and a sense of defeat to know I wasn't the only one. As I became stronger, those feelings of failure didn't return.

After the first chemotherapy, I had the Iyengar yoga teacher I've mentioned before, Jan Troy, come to the house for sessions to "rinse the organs," as she described it. Several years before, Anastasia and I had gone to a yoga week led by Karin Stephan in Sanibel, Florida. There I learned a lot about what yoga can do for the body and psyche. A good session of yoga sends relaxing chemicals to the brain and can allow the mind to be directed away from worry and anxiety. Karin, an exceptional Iyengar yoga teacher from Cambridge, Massachusetts, says, "When the nerves are strong, there is more vitality in the body. Yoga strengthens the nerves by stimulating the neuron reaction that is related to pain and calming it down. Poses based on bending, stretching or twisting the spine bring more blood to the spine and nerves. If you don't work the spine, it becomes rigid. The spine is like a bicycle chain. When you press muscles against nerves, it lubricates the nerves, like oiling the chain."

Two or three days after each chemotherapy treatment, I tended to feel wobbly and, sometimes, on the edge of nausea. Avoiding the more active poses, Jan designed a gentle series of stretching and restorative positions with a relaxing savasana pose at the end. (We omitted the English name for it, "corpse pose," for obvious reasons.) Those precious sessions calmed my nerves and energized my body, their benefits profound. The relaxation and stretching were useful because I was in bed so much, while the idea of rinsing my organs was just plain amusing. Yoga helped me take an active rather than passive stance in the face of chemo, which in turn strengthened my resolve to get through it. I did yoga throughout my chemotherapy and beyond. Today, my yoga practice is fairly well established. I try to do some poses every day, if only for ten minutes.

Summer progressed in its own way as chemotherapy continued. Friends visited, bringing picnic dinners for my kitchen or having me over to their houses. Neighbors made sure the fridge was stocked and brought the newspapers until I could drive again. Marion came for a weekend; Rick always seemed to be working in the area just after a chemo session, appearing with armfuls of flowers, bread, cheese, cold cuts and company. Philippa and Miranda visited. Great hunks of cheese and roasted chickens from Eli's in New York arrived. Not used to all the attention, the effects gently snuck up on me. I felt less of a wanderer, someone included in a specific community of people rather than just a lone member of the human race out there.

Throughout the summer my scores on two basic cancer tests, CEA and CA 125, continued to be good. These "tumor marker" tests are one of many tools used in diagnosing cancer and its progress, though neither is definitive. CEA stands for carcinoembryonic antigen, which is a protein found in many types of cells. It can be used as one of many determinants in both breast and ovarian cancers. CA 125 is also a protein found in greater concentration in tumor cells than in other cells, especially in ovarian cancer cells. My CA 125 was very low, in the right range, and the CEA was a little high, but no one was too worried.

During those months, I became a keen observer of relationships. I was in a special place then—the focus of attention, yet someone from whom very little was demanded—so I gained new perspectives on how couples interact with each other. Scrutinizing the husbands and wives around me in light of my own life story helped me see something that must have been obvious to most other people: that two people operating as a unit, if the matching is successful, have greater strength. I understood more deeply the foundations of a lasting relationship—the give-and-take, the ability to compromise, the search for common ground as both partners changed. I realized I had missed out on something wonderful and very valuable. Partnership and bonding, strengthened by intimacy, familiarity and caring, could translate into power and freedom and fulfillment. Acceptance, warts and all, is liberating, and with acceptance one is able to give more without fear of rejection. In a partnership, one has back-up. Those truths sound simple, but they had been difficult for me to truly grasp.

Sitting on my floral daybed that summer, soft pillows supporting my back and cushions propping up my legs, I would look out at the trees lining my driveway as if looking at a watercolor. They often stilled my mind from banal daily distractions, bringing me back to relaxation after overdosing on phone calls. Although a lifeline to the outside world, calls could be tiring and did not always refresh me. Given so much forced leisure and time alone, unable to do much, I was compelled to think, to prevent the summer from being a wasted opportunity to learn more about the past. I began drifting backwards, remembering moments both big and small from childhood to the present. When I had the energy or will to tackle tough issues, I managed some stocktaking. Even with therapy, I hadn't had been able to fully address some of these matters. Who were the people, what were the choices that had informed my life so far? How had I made those choices? How had they led me to where I was now?

Sometimes reality hit me hard. I came head to head with the lack of focus, almost aimlessness, underpinning certain parts of my life. I had started jobs and projects and not continued with them since my teenage years; commitment had been difficult. Led in many different directions, I had tried too many new beginnings that hadn't panned out. Career fantasies about acting or singing were for the most part just that: fantasies. Learning to act and sing had helped me grow, but I had made huge investments of time and resources in those pursuits. I knew I was intelligent and had some talent. But I realized I was disappointed in myself for not having had more of a career.

Yet, this special, quiet time alone helped me understand and better accept that the will to achieve had been knocked out of me early on, as a youngster. Despite my social poise and some of the superficial signs of belief in myself, I had lacked self-confidence. In the end, the work I did alone from May to September penetrated deeper than the effects of chemo. I was searching for a new identity—for new grounding, even without having been that sure of what the old one was.

The depth and extent of these reflections surprised me. The aftereffects of cancer surgery with respect to sexuality, sensuality, bones, heart, or other personal matters had not been part of my doctors' pre-op conversations. The goals of orthodox treatment are life extension and possible cure. Quality of life and the joy of living are not really emphasized in conventional treatment, other than doctors and nurses keeping a positive outlook from moment to moment. I was now pointedly aware that lives can radically, irrevocably change on a dime. My concerns that I had been stuck in the past, never quite able to leave it behind, rankled. When was I going to be happy? What would it depend on? How long does it have to take? Did I have enough treasure already in family, in nature, and in spirit to find what I needed? Did I know what I needed, other than more joy in my life? I told myself to accept that I could never recreate the past and had no more time to work on that. Living well from now on, indeed, would be the very best revenge, as would the talent to cherish each day, if I could. I would try.

I reached out to the past, seeking all the positive connections rather than dwelling on failures. I remembered my best friend from boarding school, Nonie Wyckoff, whom I had not seen or talked to for years. I had adored her family, especially her mother, and loved visiting their house on Lake Muskoka in Canada. When I contacted her, Nonie was surprised to hear from me, but our conversation bubbled on as if time had stood still. She told me she was going on a cruise that would leave from Fort Lauderdale later in September. I was touched when she asked me if I'd like to join her, picking up from forty years before as if we had never lost touch.

Taking an ocean voyage, relaxing with a dear friend from the past, enjoying a bit of pampering and some take-it-or-leave-it physical exertion felt like the perfect ending to my four months of travails. But the timing presented a challenge. My final chemo session coincided with the ship's boarding date in Florida. I obviously couldn't be in two places at once, never mind the fatigue following the sessions. When I presented this to Karen and Lisa, the chemo nurses, they bent over backwards to work things out. They had been watching me, checking both my blood work and reactions to the chemo. They believed I did not need the last chemo session and that it might even do more harm than good. Fortunately, Dr. Schwartz trusts his nurses, so a couple of days after those arrangements had been made, he cancelled the final chemotherapy session. It was almost an anti-climax: I was done.

"Check-ups every three months with a physical exam and tumor marker tests for a year," I was told. "After a year, it's every six months, and then every year for the same tests and a mammogram." That was it. I said goodbye with a sense of gratitude. The nurses had been wonderful: caring, careful and strong. I handed out some little gifts to my helpers before I bounced out the revolving doors of the Physician's Building, enjoying having the freedom to drive myself home this time. Then, I started packing for the cruise. For now, I put serious questions aside. I would laugh and have fun with my old friend. Now, how many suitcases would I need for the boat?

10

All There Is

It's never too late – in fiction or in life – to revise.
— NANCY THAYER

When you are dealing with a serious illness, you inhabit a different time zone than other people. Things seem to move in slow motion. Cancer had moved me outside any mainstream I believed I had inhabited and into another dimension, a parallel universe consisting of my time only. But "real" time did pass. Suddenly it was September, and the unusual attention I had been getting slowed. Dale had moved on to other patients; doctors and nurses no longer called. Though still caring and concerned, the wonderful friends who had seen me through the summer were getting back to their daily lives as before. The girls believed I'd recovered. They had a full plate of tasks themselves. John had been great, but now that my crisis was over, I was more and more aware that he was involved with someone else, a younger woman who had been in his life for several years.

All that summer I had looked out on a friendly but solitary landscape: two curving, parallel lines of young beeches rolling down my rutted, gravel driveway with new grass on either side, the trees healthy and verdant, adaptable and enduring. Youth was on their side; when I looked at them I saw survival. Some days, nothing in that view moved. At other times, the trees seemed to reach out to me, as if telling me not to worry, it would be all right. I would be a survivor, too.

Now, the end of summer had stealthily crept up on me. My trees had lost their full summer verdure. Their leaves had begun to change color and crisp up, no longer in the flush of youth. The summer season of ripeness and expansion was drawing to its close. I couldn't help drawing a parallel to myself. Had my season of expansion done the same?

Worrying that what had happened so far in my life might have been "it," I reviewed my biography. Had "it" been "enough"? A moment earlier in the year sprang to mind: catching my face in a mirror in the ladies room at City Opera. Rushing to get back to my seat before the second act curtain and off guard, I had been shocked to find a mask of sadness and discontent reflected back at me. Not only in the downturned corners of my mouth but my eyes transmitted that same message. All said to me, "You are not a happy woman."

In the midst of these emotional reflections, worries about health nagged. Cancer had marked me, both for good and for ill. Surgery, chemo poisons, baldness, the loss of organs, as well as fear and loneliness had mercilessly carved their signature onto and through me, periodically jabbing at the less optimistic side of my nature. My unquestioning faith that life would always provide the right path had been shaken. Could I ever regain what I thought I had been, healthy and robust, living without having to pace myself constantly? Would the endless worrying about cancer and recurrence ever go away? I accepted that a new chapter in my life had opened, one with an unfamiliar name tag: cancer survivor. It was an achievement, but the "survivor" part still often felt either doubtful or ambiguous.

I wasn't Humpty Dumpty, so I was sure the physical pieces could be put back together again. But that September, I realized more and more clearly that other sorts of repairs were in order—to both body and psyche, but mostly psyche. Another rebuilding effort faced me, probably even more strenuous than previous ones. This came as a huge, daunting surprise. I would have to return to the drawing board to figure it all out yet again.

Another event that fall cast an ominous pall. One morning in early September, John and I were driving into New York, the radio on WINS for the traffic news, when the announcer reported that a small plane had hit one of the twin towers at the World Trade Center. Out the car window to the left, a spiral of black smoke rose in the clear blue sky. September 11th inflicted a wound to the national soul as well as to mine. Two days later, Nonie called to say that our trip was cancelled. Her cousin, married to the (then) chair of the House Intelligence Committee, Porter Goss, had called to say she must not go on the cruise as planned. There were reports of other possible attacks and Americans were at risk, he counselled. I had been looking forward to the respite, but the cancellation made sense. It would have been counterproductive, to say the least, to go on a trip to forget my terror only to be surrounded by a more general fear.

As a sort of consolation prize, John offered to take me on a road trip. We would leave New York and head to Sea Island, Georgia, somewhere neither of us had ever been. He later admitted, under pressure, that it was an act of duty, an obligation to help the wounded. He was disappointed for me that I'd miss the sea voyage. Today, I remember that journey as so weird it almost defies description, the most detached rendezvous of our more than twenty-five year relationship.

I was still in my turban, but little sprouts of hair were peeking out and my eyebrows were starting to grow back one precious, coveted hair at a time. We left from New York early on a Sunday, heading south on the New Jersey turnpike. The car trip down the coast had some fun moments, especially in the Carolinas. There, we found a rinky-dink road house where we gorged on boiled shrimp served with brown bread and red salt, downing beer and watching football on the TV in the bar. We drove to the Outer Banks, saw where the Wright Brothers had taken off, looked at lighthouses and stopped at a romantic little hotel on the water. Through it all John seemed present in body only, an ambivalent and off-putting companion. I still remember the sense I had during our return, somewhere around exit nine on the

New Jersey Turnpike, of feeling John's detachment sucking up the available oxygen in his car. When we reached the city, I was politely yet unceremoniously dropped back where I was staying. After that, I didn't see much of him for a while, which hurt me.

Even before the trip, I was puzzling over our on-off relationship. I had married him, divorced him, and was kind of seeing him again. At best, it was confusing for both of us. At that time, there was so much to think about that I couldn't figure out what we were or what we should be to each other. I think he was having the same problem. A big fork in the road loomed out in front of me. I couldn't decide which direction to take, or even what the choices were. I was quite lost, unable to define exactly why, stuck, in stasis. The good news was that I was beginning to comprehend some of the bigger missing parts in my history, like an enduring relationship with a partner or a card-carrying membership in a community. With that understanding came an upsetting awareness of loss.

Another memory came back to taunt me, a sister to that moment in front of the ladies' room mirror. Many years before, a friend in London had asked if I really knew who I was. I fudged the answer to the question, which I found too invasive. My hold on my identity was none of her darn business. But what she said had rankled and been stashed away in my head. Lying on my Connecticut daybed, I was finally ready to concede that she'd had a point. Outside of a social identity and work resume, motherhood and cancer were my marks. Other parts needed development. Therapy had gotten me to third base; it was time for a home run, a final separation from the damage of the past.

I had no idea of how to accomplish this. I had run out of shrinks and marriage counsellors. I'd even run temporarily out of energy. By mid-fall neither my hair, eyebrows nor vitality had snapped back to past, or even acceptable, levels. I had always been able to summon the energy to do anything I wanted or needed to do–John often described me as being "driven." At this juncture, I had to budget all available vigor.

Finally driving again, I found myself communicating with my car through my foot. I was more aware and careful behind the wheel than I had ever been before. Going too fast had been a lifelong habit, but now the Audi was feeling like too much automobile for me. It felt like a metaphor for parts of my life. My new alter ego, my car, agreed. "From now on," she told me, "you are going to go slower, and you'll enjoy that gentler pace. And lady, this has nothing to do with energy levels; this has to do with how you're going to live from now on. You have been going too fast, for too long, to nowhere. You're not always so good at listening but maybe it's time to pay attention to how *I* want this car to drive."

I tried to listen. For the rest of the autumn, the alter-ego Audi and I drove in and out of New York, seeing friends both there and in Connecticut. Candidly, I don't really recall all that much about that period, except a widening feeling of loneliness—a sense that my house was expanding around me, growing too large. Months after chemo had been pronounced a success, I still felt confused about life's direction. I only knew I craved a life that would let me integrate all the hard-fought changes I had struggled to make before the illness. So I demanded one more very big step, that of fully regaining every aspect of my health—to include body, mind and spirit or soul. I was judiciously seeking a more perfect health, a *balanced* health, for the first time.

I considered options. Complementary medicine and therapies such as chiropractic, yoga and acupuncture had always appealed to me, but were already part of my routine. I'd had positive experiences with a homeopathic physician and an applied kinesiologist, but intuition told me clearly that just adding those back into my life wouldn't accomplish the big transformation I was seeking.

Then a light bulb snapped on. One of my "stalwarts"—the kind of friend you want in a crisis as well as at dinner—is a woman named Patricia Sullivan. Intelligent, wise and exceedingly good company, she has many interesting connections and manoeuvres successfully in several different worlds. Pattie sits on the board of an organization called the Marion Institute, founded by her friend Michael Baldwin. In 1998 the Institute had arranged a visit by a Swiss physician, Dr. Thomas Rau, to the National Academy of Sciences in New York. Always generous in sharing her knowledge, Pattie invited many of her friends to go hear Dr. Rau speak about the form of medicine he practiced, Biological Medicine.

Margie and Michael Baldwin had found Dr. Rau after their son Nathaniel had endured myriad cancer treatments, including bone marrow replacement. They were told that Nathaniel would always have some disabilities, including a permanent loss of over 50% of lung function, but they refused to accept the hopelessness of that diagnosis. Wide searches discovered the Paracelsus Clinic in Switzerland. Nathaniel made several visits to the clinic in Lustmuhle, and under Dr. Rau's care, he regained over 95% of his lung function. His overall progress was so significant that the Baldwins were eager to make Dr. Rau's practices better known in the United States.

I had been a little late to that 1998 seminar, and was shepherded into an adjacent room which had only a monitor with poor sound reproduction. Though I could hardly hear Dr. Rau, he was nonetheless impressive. Passion, commitment and even joy lit up this doctor from Switzerland as he spoke of his healing work. When he said, "Illness is the expression of a fundamental imbalance in the human being," it had hit a bull's eye in my mind. I had felt that kind of imbalance. Now I came to the fork in the road: to find a new balance, or go on as before.

I remembered Dr. Rau explaining that Biological Medicine emphasizes the detoxification of the body and de-acidification of the cells, tissues, and the "milieu," a key component. The milieu is the total inner environment of our bodies, including the extra-cellular fluid that carries oxygen and nutrients to the body tissues, carries waste out, and helps keep us balanced and healthy. This form of medicine strives to create a more alkaline environment for the milieu. Unlike practitioners of orthodox Western medicine, the clinic treated the whole person, not just individual organs or diseases. "We treat the person, not the illness," said Dr. Rau, adding that the individual is seen as a dynamic, ever-changing entity.

The memory of that talk energized me, giving me a direction. Pattie told me how to get in touch with the Baldwins and the Paracelsus Clinic. I discovered that Dr. Rau would be conducting a weekend workshop in Massachusetts in December and I quickly signed up. In the meantime, I tried to learn more about my cancer, cells in general, and the Paracelsus Clinic.

Paracelsus was a celebrated but controversial sixteenth-century physician, astrologer, reformer, and (like most of the practicing physicians of the time) alchemist who travelled and studied all over Europe. Seeking to overturn some of the conventional thinking of the time and to find what makes people get sick, he pioneered the use of chemicals and minerals in medicine, introduced the study of toxicology, and gave zinc its name. Much of what he and his contemporaries believed would be considered antiquated now. But his conviction that healing could be assisted by a change in diet was far ahead of its time, given that the best cancer research today speaks of diet and exercise as the two main factors in cancer prevention. He believed everything in the universe was interrelated and that illness is caused by imbalances in the body. After learning all that, I understood why the clinic was named after this 16th century pioneer of the healing arts.

It wasn't the deciding factor, but the simple fact that the clinic's location was in Switzerland had positive associations for me. The Swiss had many clinics, a reputation for good medicine, and the freedom to use healing treatments that would not be allowed in the United States. But there was a more personal, deeper resonance as well. When I had left Switzerland back in June of 1958, an inner voice had whispered, "You'll be back." Evidently, that omniscient, sly inner voice had known something of my future that I didn't. Over the years, I had wondered when and why going back would happen, sensing that the reason would be more important than tourism or some other frivolous purpose. Most of us have prophetic insights at times, some knowledge about our lives that we haven't yet accessed or explored. It seems we know more than we know that we know. Now, more than 40 years after leaving, I welcomed the thought of returning to a country I had loved. I had felt safe and cared for there. Switzerland felt like the perfect place to heal a body rendered frail with damaging cocktails of anaesthetics and anti-cancer drugs.

While I was evaluating all this, I went to Florida to visit Nonie and another friend from school. One of Dr. Rau's patients lived nearby. She invited me to come and talk to her about the clinic. A distinguished woman and accomplished artist, she turned out to be smart, helpful and a pivotal figure for me. She thought highly of the clinic and the benefits I would accrue there. As we talked, I was on the verge of tears several times. The experience of the past months welled up in the presence of this empathic spirit. She seemed so on top of things, making me conscious that I wasn't. My tears were tears of relief and release. I felt relief at meeting someone who had personally experienced what I was about to, and the release that comes from being able to let go with someone who really understood anguish and fear.

She loaned me the diary she had written during one of her stays at the clinic, telling me to keep it for a few days. It was an extraordinary gesture, especially as the journal revealed personal details about her life.

At the end of our meeting, she looked into my eyes and said, "You have a lot of work to do." I didn't know quite how to take that at the time. Now I do. She also mentioned an astrologer, someone she knew of who would do a comprehensive astrological chart for me. She felt that this could help me understand myself better. Mother had often taken me along when she went to Miss Madeleine, who read the tea leaves upstairs, somewhere on Madison Avenue, way back in the early sixties. I think she was hoping to see her next husband in the crystal ball. But my new acquaintance appeared to be a more down-to-earth woman, so I took Steven Forrest's telephone number and contacted him. Requesting the "Transitions" reading she had suggested for me, I learned that the results would arrive in January, as there was a backlog.

By early December, I felt certain I would give Dr. Rau and his clinic a try. Since I still needed information—reassurance that this was the right step—I was excited to get in the Audi and drive to the doctor's seminar in Marion, Massachusetts.

It was a weekend affair geared to professionals and other interested parties designed to explain some of the finer points of this unique form of treatment. Dr. Rau looked much like I remembered him from that earlier talk, tall and slender, a man who exuded energy and focus, with steel-rimmed glasses and a gaze that was strong, but kind. I was able to speak to and question him briefly, but though he answered helpfully he was too busy at that time to answer in detail. He was explaining complicated principles and theories to a room packed with professionals, and I thought it best to listen and to learn.

I was fascinated by Dr. Rau's ideas about the more complete health that could arise by moving beyond "symptoms" and changing not just physical health but also one's spiritual and inner life. He reinforced my first impression of him as a dedicated professional, passionate about his subject. It intrigued me that this trained rheumatologist had arrived at such a sophisticated, holistic form of treatment through listening to his patients when they said that acupuncture or homeopathy made them feel better than his orthodox methods. The simple fact that he had listened and then changed his practices grabbed my attention, telling me he was not only honest and humble but also someone who didn't always have to be right. Dr. Rau's willingness to change in order to find better solutions was a big plus for me, perhaps because it mirrored what I was trying to do in my own life.

That December, I spoke to a few people who had been to the clinic and were pleased with their treatment. No surprise, because they'd agreed to be interviewed, but their reactions were clearly sincere. They emphasized that everyone's program was specially tailored, though mentioned that they had all had dental work for reasons I didn't yet understand.

How do we make these important decisions that we hope will change our lives for the better? This decision was more than a hunch;

I'd call it intuition with back-up. The right "fork in the road" was turning into the only road. I would be inspected with a fine-tooth comb, diagnosed for both weaknesses and strengths, and exhaustively treated. New issues emerging from test results would be addressed as well.

Finally, I just said to myself that I had all the information I needed. I would go. I had good vibes about it, and that was that. Leaving Marion after the seminar, I signed up for three weeks of testing, treatments, dental work and talk therapy beginning in March, the earliest they could take me. For a first-time patient with a cancer diagnosis, three weeks is the recommended stay, partly to allow for the delay between testing and receiving the results. Though I'd had cancer, this would be an overall treatment for wellness and detoxification. I felt lucky to be able to afford it, and knew that was a privilege not everyone enjoyed. I believe the beginning of my work as an advocate for preventative medicine and healthy aging was forged at this time.

I was surprised the clinic requested only a family history and information regarding my illness, not seeming to care that much about all the hospital reports. I wrote it all out, including past illnesses, my personal history, and as much information about parents and grandparents as was available, plus a brief description of the cancer, the surgery and the treatments afterwards. The emphasis here, on providing my own narrative rather than relying entirely on medical records, was already different from that of most practitioners of Western medicine. It reminded me of the extensive questions asked by the homeopath in Connecticut I'd visited years before. The power of telling one's own story shouldn't be underestimated; the act of claiming and expressing one's experience has a potent value of its own. By the time I sent off the $250 deposit, I already felt engaged in my future and empowered by the direct approach I'd taken. That done, I didn't dither too much regarding the *pros* or the *cons*.

Christmas approached with the exciting prospect of a visit from both of the girls at once. Anastasia was coming from London with Stefan. Philippa, her husband John and their daughter, Miranda, would drive down from Pawtucket, Rhode Island. It was wonderful to think we'd all be together. Anastasia and Stefan arrived in New York. They stayed with John, who took them out to dinner to welcome them to the Big Apple. Though he and the girls were close, John was otherwise involved over this holiday period. I was disappointed when he told me not to count on seeing him over Christmas at all.

Anastasia, Stefan and I went to a couple of New York parties, saw *La Bohème* at the Met, and then decamped for Connecticut after picking up a suckling pig at one of New York's best butchers, Albert's. By the time we left New York, the car was so packed with stuff we looked like the Beverly Hillbillies.

Christmas turned out to be nicely uneventful, relaxing and quiet. It was a bit sad to not see John at all. As the year came to a close we couldn't help but think of other sadnesses, too, including the country's 9/11 wounds and the possibility of a war ahead. But we loved all the music of Christmas, from Handel's *Messiah* and carol singing from King's College, Cambridge, to Bing Crosby renditions. We kept them blaring on the sound system while we read, cooked and ate delicious meals. We stoked lots of fires in the hearth, and there was even a little snow on the ground. Another very bright spot was having Miranda in the house. Now a robust eight-month-old, she spent a night in my room, good as gold of course.

Preparations for our Christmas dinner were skillfully executed by both daughters and their partners. My job was to place the apple in the pig's mouth and set the table, alive and festive with red napkins, candles and Christmas Crackers with their snappers brought from England. Anastasia and Stefan went to the late church service. Not up to giving the annual Christmas party I had thrown in the past, we all went to a friend's annual post-Christmas cocktail gathering, the whole town swept into an old colonial house with creaky floorboards and crackling fires.

I mentioned my plans for the Paracelsus Clinic to the girls, presenting it as a great opportunity. They were happy, especially if I was. With that, Christmas 2001 came to a close. Though the holiday had its somber moments, nothing could have been better than having all my family with me.

After receiving all the confirmations from the clinic, I booked the overnight flight to Zurich. The clinic was outpatient only, so lodging was a necessity as well. I reserved a room at a *pension*—a small, family-run boarding house—in the tiny nearby village of Teufen. Called the Schutzengarten, the hotel was recommended for clinic patients as it offered Dr. Rau's alkalinizing diet. It would become a familiar place to me, and was a place that many of us frequent visitors to the clinic came to both love and to hate.

The early part of 2002 seemed to pass amid a slow-motion vortex born both of high expectations and hovering uncertainties. I had made some silly choices in life, and now that my course seemed set on Switzerland, I was having one or two small doubts about this one. A few friends didn't understand why I was going or what I was doing. I wasn't able to give a complete explanation and didn't really want to try, or go into it. Concerns cropped up through talking to other patients as the time drew nearer. Tooth extractions were mentioned again, but they weren't anything I wished to address yet either. Much had to be taken on faith, based on what I had heard in Dr. Rau's lectures as well as the responses of the sane and intelligent clinic patients I had talked to.

Then there was a revelation, the first of that year of revelations. It came in late January, when I received Steve Forrest's reading. Back then, it came on two cassettes. Diving in to it, I was absolutely riveted. He began by telling me he was looking at "my nature at birth and the condition of my soul at birth, including karmic predicaments" as well as "the future I was intending to create." He described the position of all the houses in my chart at my birth and the position of the planets, including the ascendant ones. That part of the reading was technical and complex, so I was grateful for his clear explanations.

As he explained, it seemed I was always drawn to that which undercut my certainty. He found, as he examined my past lives, that I had previously died in a state of spiritual conflict and that bad karma was following me. I was extremely sensitive, and defences and solitude are necessary to my survival. In order to go to the future, I would have to clean up the karmic past. Among other things, I shouldn't identify with things not worthy of me, and I would need methods to evolve my consciousness. "Cancerians defend themselves with shells, like the crab, today's symbol of Cancer," he said.

Sensitivity and the need for solitude were definitely part of my *modus operandi*. My report from the Little Red School House, all the way back at age four, described me as sensitive and liking to be alone. I also agreed with that karmic insight. I didn't know, or really care, how he'd arrived at the past life information, but I did know that my whole life had been about cleaning up the past. Here was someone telling me to do it.

The Paracelsus Clinic's information pack had told me that they did work, based on the teachings of the late Rudolf Steiner, that would investigate not only the body but the mind, soul and spirit to boot. Steven's reading perfectly aligned with that. I felt more and more optimistic that this was a new beginning, one that would allow me to find the deep healing I'd been seeking for so long.

Still, not everyone agreed, even among those I most trusted. A few days before departure, I had a friendly verbal tussle with my beloved general practitioner, John Postley. As I've mentioned before, John is a gem, one of the smartest and most sensitive doctors one could ever meet. I always checked medical things with him, especially if I was scared of a test result (usually a tumor marker that was slightly high) or something else that didn't feel right. After cancer, even a hangnail could get me somewhat upset, at least until a couple of years passed, enough time for me to start losing the fear. Trust is essential in medical relationships, and I have always trusted in John Postley's calm wisdom, common sense, and professional acumen. He is my chief rabbi, general contractor and Pope. In fact, if there is ever a Mephistophelean struggle in my head over whether I am well or not, I will rely on John and John (Horn and Postley) to bring me to calm.

But John Postley is an allopathic doctor. His medicine looks for measurable illness detectable in the body, the orthodox approach. Though he isn't opposed to alternative therapy, he remains sceptical of some of its practices as well as the intrinsic value of many of the treatments. Now, he suggested that since I was well, no longer being treated for cancer, why should I go to Europe for treatment? It was hard to go against his disapproval. But I did it, sticking to my guns. We had a laugh as I agreed to come in and see him upon my return.

My talk with Dr. Postley clarified something essential in my mind. Curing and healing may sound like the same thing, but our discussion underscored that for me, they were very different. To be completely healed, I felt that both emotional and physical components had to be involved. Healing connoted a sense of restoration, including a balanced spiritual dimension and value system. In contrast, curing—a more clinic term—just meant you were fixed, that the illness or its symptoms were over.

I knew that for now, I'd travelled as far as I could with conventional treatments. Tough as chemotherapy had turned out to be, I had few regrets. But though my illness was technically over, I knew that something was definitely missing, well beyond a couple of body parts. My internal balance, my whole self, including my soul and emotions, had needed adjusting even before cancer, the treatment and its residual toxins. Business as usual wouldn't be enough to push my reset button.

Philippa offered to come down to Connecticut to help me get ready for the trip. A superb packer, she can give you three reasons why you should bring the maroon pants (which you might have considered a fourth-place-maybe) and not the gray flannels; evaluate all of the other stuff you are appraising; and get everything into one reasonable-size suitcase, leaving extra room for presents. She was extremely tough when it came to shoes, resisting my impulse to bring all of my favorites. In addition to limiting my luggage to manageable size, we had to tackle the issue of outerwear. March would be chilly in Switzerland, even more so because the clinic was at high altitude. I was pleased by the final choice, a mid-length, tan shearling coat and a scarf that wasn't too contrived.

Michael Condon, a retired businessman doing airport gigs, came over late in that March afternoon. As we piled into the Audi and departed for Kennedy Airport, I watched the the landscape I knew so well pass by with a distinct sense that I was leaving much more behind than familiar scenery.

11

Return to Switzerland

Sometime in your life you will go on a long journey. It will be the longest journey you have ever
taken. It is the journey to find yourself.
— KATHERINE SHARP

On the plane, finally relaxing with a glass of wine and dinner after
the rush of departure and airport security, I began to consider this
return to Switzerland from a different perspective. The privacy and
anonymity of the vast aircraft allowed me to be more in step with my
emotions, letting me "sit" more quietly with the many feelings that
had been swirling within me over the past weeks.

I had brought the clinic's information packet with me, and I took
some time to re-read that as well. I paid special attention to the material about Dr. Hans-Heinrich Reckeweg, a German doctor who eventually settled in the United States in the 1970s. Dr. Reckeweg tried to
bridge allopathic and homeopathic medicine with a line of remedies
he developed himself. His system had become an important part of
the clinic's work.

His theory is based on the belief that when the body is working
well, all of its complex systems work together to ensure the efficient
excretion of toxins and waste. When these self-regulatory capacities
in the body start to break down, inflammation occurs and the system
is forced to excrete more dramatically. If we medicate ourselves with

things like antibiotics and steroids, which only suppress symptoms, or follow a poor diet without exercise, a downward spiral begins. Toxins that can't be eliminated are stored in tissue, resulting in deepening problems that may become chronic or even fatal. Dr. Reckeweg's understanding and description of the inflammatory process is quite different from that which most of us have been taught. But it served the clinic's unique approach—and ultimately my own health needs as well. The concept made sense to me.

With Swiss precision, the plane landed on time in Zurich early on Sunday morning, March 3. I made it through the baggage claim and looked for my ride. I didn't know the ropes back then, so I had treated myself to a taxi for the hour-plus trip from the airport to Lustmuhle. It was expensive, but worth it that first time. Now I take the train, one of the most efficient and clean transportation systems in the world. You could almost eat off the floors; they are pristine.

The taxi passed through a cloudy, sunless city, quiet and Calvinist, as church bells expressed their awareness of a brand new day. Rising a dozen miles to the south, the Alps are visible on a good day, glorious and majestic, but they stayed clothed in mist that Sunday. In Zurich, prosperity leaks out of every pore, every automobile, every butcher and every restaurant; the streets are as clean as a well-scrubbed sink. Even the dogs and cats look prosperous.

As we arrived in Teufen, the sun appeared briefly. No one seemed to be at the Schutzengarten when I arrived but eventually Irene and Christian Guler, the proprietors, emerged from the kitchen and offered a warm greeting. The "Schutzi" is built in traditional chalet style: little hearts carved into green shutters, geraniums displayed in each window box of the hotel's façade. Yet it was March, and quite a cold one. Only later did it click that the flowers were all plastic. They gave the place a cosy look regardless. Most patients choose the Schutzi because the hotel does follow Dr. Rau's diet and is reasonably priced. Irene cooks, while Christian looks after the place and acts as concierge and porter. Irene does things with tofu and soy milk one could never imagine, while Christian hums constantly in a Switzerdeutsch lilt and believes we live in the best of all possible worlds. Together, they create an inviting and gentle atmosphere. Something about the Switzerdeutsch language, a Swiss version of German, makes it softer on the ears than regular German, adding to the poetry of the place.

Not knowing the layout when I booked my room, I had treated myself to what was called a suite. It had felt important to have a separate space without visual distractions, away from mundane 'stuff' like hairbrushes and dirty laundry—an uncluttered place for reflection and meditation. Humming and chatting away, Christian took me and my suitcase upstairs, depositing all in Room 4. The bedroom had a monastic slice of a bed and a dresser. Next to it was a spacious extra room. The duvet, my nemesis, was there glaring at me, disappointing but expected. My feet always seemed to find themselves outside the duvet, either too hot or too cold. My choice would have been white cotton sheets, crisp and fresh, and blankets to allow my beloved layering. The bathroom held a rose-colored tub and a white sink, but no toilet. I would have to go outside, into the hall for that, as is often true of *pensions* in Europe. This was a step up from the other rooms, none of which had bathtubs, an essential amenity to me.

These days, the Gulers have moved on and run a more efficient small hotel, formerly a motel. Inexpensive and full of art donated by a grateful patient and art dealer, it's the clinic's official place to lodge. Unfortunately, the duvets that made me feel nearly demented are still there, but Irene's cooking just about makes up for them.

On that first day, I looked around, unpacked a little, and then descended the narrow stairwell in search of coffee and food. The mountain air had made me hungry and it was getting towards lunch time. A Tibetan sand tray in the small lobby caught my eye. Using the miniature rake for luck, I scraped a circular design in the sand, hoping the design was karmically acceptable. Then I searched for Irene. The Schutzi didn't open for meals on a Sunday, but Irene offered to show me a restaurant where I could have brunch. It was one of the village's several food emporiums, which often include a front-of-the-store seduction in chocolate. This restaurant-*patisserie* had chocolate bunnies, marzipan carrots and other confections made in preparation for the Easter religious holiday, all beautifully tied up in purple and yellow ribbons and cellophane. The Swiss have a thing about ribbons and flowers. They never seem to rush when wrapping a bouquet or *gateau*, taking time to create the perfect bow, forming the crinkly wrapping into just the right shape.

Switzerland was and is still a religious country, primarily Calvinist and Catholic. The cows continue to get blessed at a certain point in the year. I can attest to the fact that church bells are a staple of life at all hours of the day and night, yet are strangely comforting in their assured regularity.

I can't remember what dinner was that evening. I must have foraged for something to eat and probably had a last glass of red wine before starting the clinic's mandated "rehab." I had never kept a journal, but had bought one for this stay. I wanted to be both a scribbler and an artist, taking it all in. I didn't trust my memory to preserve the finer points. My chemo-induced brain fog was still there. My journal was actually an unlined sketch book. As the lady in Florida had made such a beautiful diary, I had thought I'd try to draw as well as write. It was a fanciful notion given a sorry lack of artistic talent, somewhat akin to trying to create a *sacher torte* from a pound of Mars Bars. I sketched my room, wasn't overly impressed, and only scribbled from then on.

A printed schedule for my first few days at the clinic had been left at the hotel. I learned that there could often be changes, so only a few days were given at a time. The schedule sheet gave the date, time, duration, location and type of treatment as well as the doctor's name, unless the procedure was to be executed by a technician or nurse. A blue file held both schedule and a brief description of what the treatments would be. Nothing I read that first day put up a red flag. I'd heard of colonics, saunas and x-rays, and I decided that what I didn't understand wasn't worth fretting about at this point. I had already accepted that this course of treatment would be very different from anything I'd previously experienced. In addition, I figured it couldn't be worse than chemo. It was obvious there would be a learning curve, with some things that would be difficult to understand. But my research had convinced me that Dr. Rau had helped many people. I just had to trust that he would help me, too.

I felt hopeful and enthusiastic as I started my three weeks at Paracelsus. Early on that Monday, the obligatory dental x-rays were done, everyone's starting point. Nothing else would happen until Tuesday at 8:30 a.m. when I would meet with Dr. Rau for the first time. After the comprehensive x-rays that Monday, I was free for the rest of the day. In the village, I climbed on the famous little red "choo-choo" train, so tiny it looks like a toy, with no conductor and only two cars. I took it to the end of the line, a picture-book Swiss village called Appenzell at the foot of the mountains. To be near the mountains again in Switzerland was like a homecoming, filling me with nostalgia. Unable to resist the Swiss cheese made in that very town, I stopped at the hotel restaurant in the square. I indulged in a lunch of a salad and a wedge of nutty Appenzell cheese, cut from a huge cheese wheel, along with a glass of Swiss fondant—a light, crisp white wine, not often exported. Sitting on the terrace of the chalet-style hotel, watching the bustling waitresses dressed in dirndl dresses and enjoying the sun, I felt only gratitude.

On the way back I got off at Schattl, about a mile from the Schutzengarten. From there I walked along the top of a hill, looking down at the villages below, following the *wanderweg* signs. Passionate walkers and outdoor people, the Swiss have provided a comprehensive network of path markers, whose arrows pointing in different directions give the traveller precise distances and clear directions; it's hard to get lost. A feeling of joy overtook me as I walked, all hopes rekindled. To be back in Switzerland, to have the chance to heal, to learn more about my body and to pursue real health were great reasons to celebrate.

I was being proactive in the truest sense, taking action before another event occurred, pre-empting possible threats, which in my case could have included a recurrence of cancer. I had taken things lying down from June until mid-September, submitting to and believing in the protocol designed by Dr. Schwartz. Now, I was placing my faith in Dr. Rau and his kind of treatment, very different but for me, "just what the doctor ordered" for this phase of my life.

Back at the hotel, I ran a hot bath, soaked in pine oil, and decided to venture down to dinner. I wondered whom I'd find, not completely sure I was ready to socialize. The chalet-style dining room was sweet and rustic, complete with more designs carved into the wooden interior shutters. Irene's cooking turned out to be delicious and almost completely vegetarian except on Fridays, when a token piece of fish or a chicken stew might appear. A large refectory table sat about twenty people; a few banquette tables lining one of the walls completed the room. Thick white paper tablecloths and red paper napkins accompanied fresh little bouquets of flowers and pitchers of room-temperature water, as the clinic did not consider ice water good for either the organs or the cells. It was immaculate and inviting.

Someone called out an invitation to sit at the big table. I joined about twelve other guests, all chattering away about their treatments, their condition and their weekend—what nurse they particularly liked, the foibles of this or that doctor. It was a very congenial group, mostly from the United States, so I felt welcome and comfortable. It was also an introduction to the clinic's approaches and philosophies, as seen through other patients' eyes.

Not everyone staying at the Schutzi had cancer. There were cases of multiple sclerosis, neurofibromyalgia, liver disease, type-C hepatitis, mercury poisoning, and other diverse complaints. Three women who did have cancer and were being treated for the disease were quite serious ongoing cases. Most of the cancer patients I ultimately met there had already been through the chemo/radiation mill, usually with results showing a poor prognosis. Others had come because they had rejected standard treatments from the start, wanting a solely holistic protocol. Some patients had been told by the allopathic medical community that everything possible had been done—that they were terminal cases with little hope. In other words, the clinic received many patients whose cases are very advanced and hard to treat, and for whom it would be difficult to obtain good results. Dr. Rau's work is considered controversial, even though he is a medical doctor licensed to lecture in the United States. His approach is out of line with mainstream, conventional thinking, which is mostly concerned with measurable symptoms and has less emphasis on treating the whole person. Nevertheless, even the most medically challenged patients I met at the clinic (like those I had talked to before coming to Switzerland) were optimistic about their treatments there.

That first night I met Helena, a remarkable woman. Young, blonde and slim, she had large tumors pushing out of both her face and her neck, seeming to grow almost before my eyes. Because these growths made it difficult to swallow, she had to chew slowly. Helena felt guilty for keeping people waiting at dinner, so she would leave the table to continue her meal upstairs while waiting for her children to call. Her dignity and spirit made it more than humbling to watch her. A couple from California were there to treat the wife's breast cancer, a recurrence. She had tumors growing on the outside of her breasts and apparently they were seeping. It sounded ghastly. Understandably depressed, her Greg was a real stalwart, endlessly tender with her, infusing her with enough hope for both of them.

Another woman at the refectory table was an American screenwriter living in France, recently married to a younger Italian. She was lively, pretty and full of gallows humor. She had Hepatitis C, so she was sure her days were numbered. Childless, she was speculating who her "Italian stallion" would marry next, and how her money would be spent and on whom.

Lorraine Hunt Lieberson was also there for breast cancer, from which I learned that her sister had died. A famous mezzo-soprano at the height of her powers at that time, Lorraine opted not to have chemo or radiation, since no physician could predict with any certainty what such treatments might do to her voice. A first-class diva, kind and charming, brave and fragile, she did very well for many years under Dr. Rau's care. Though her stay, one of many, was winding down as I arrived, we had many talks before her departure. As she left, she handed me her own copy of a little book of Buddhist sayings by the American-Tibetan monk Pema Chodron. The pages Lorraine had bent down were well-thumbed, mostly concerned with detachment and goodness. Lorraine died in July 2006, leaving behind an international career, large numbers of people who miss her deeply, and the admiration of opera lovers everywhere. It was said of her, "When Lorraine sang, time itself stopped to listen." I can well believe it.

Peter Lieberson, Lorraine's husband, turned out to be very helpful. When we started talking about the dental work performed at the clinic, he intelligently explained some of the whys and wherefores of Dr. Rau's ideas. Peter's explanation of the importance of the teeth and the use of traditional Chinese and Ayurvedic medicine gave me clearer insights into the thinking of the clinic. The diagnostics of both those systems are based on extensive observation. They look at the entire health picture of the patient, including emotions, physical constitution and behavior. Philippa, Anastasia and Stefan called during dinner, as did John and Marion Bedrick; I had to leave the table and the tooth conversation several times. Peter assured me that we could talk again. That was a relief, as I was sure I would have more questions.

I'd had a wonderful evening. I'd enjoyed a good dinner with interesting people, including some who were very sick. I'd heard from friends and family. With jet lag setting in, I was ready to call it a day. On my way up to bed, my reassurance level about being in Switzerland had risen even higher. That Dr. Rau's reputation had reached so far and wide, often by word of mouth, made a solid impression on me. Those dinner guests who were return patients, like Lorraine and Peter, were fully convinced of Dr. Rau's methods. My decision to be treated was not only being reinforced, but beginning to look pretty smart.

Brushing my teeth with new found care, I pondered what might be in store for me regarding my two root canals. The one in my front tooth had been done when I was fourteen. Now discoloured, it was a very old bit of dentistry. But I had done enough thinking and weighing for one night. Mercifully I fell asleep, pesky duvet and all.

12

Explorations

If we don't change, we don't grow. If we don't grow,
we aren't really living.

— GAIL SHEEHY

Tuesday was my first complete day at the clinic. It began with Irene's
breakfast of a single-grain porridge (the clinic doesn't mix grains) and
some dinkle bread. Dinkle is what we call spelt in English—in its
ancient form, a wheat high in fiber and minerals. A bit of butter was
allowed with it, since butter is viewed, remarkably, not as a dairy
product but only as a fat.

Chewing slowly in an attempt to make a good beginner's start, I
ran my mind over the day's schedule. After meeting Dr. Rau, I would
have blood tests, a meeting with the clinic's "concierge," and a variety
of appointments, among which were: the gynecologist; an x-ray of the
thorax; an infra-red sauna (which I took to mean just a sauna) and an
HRI, whatever that was.

This series is the standard opening act for a stay at Paracelsus, the
basic diagnostic tests and treatments performed to create a more
comprehensive picture of the patient, outside of and away from symptoms. The focus is on treating the whole person, in addition to treating any conditions and complaints patients arrive with. Treatments
are then personalized according to the patient's state of overall health,

with the doctors always searching for the root causes of problems. Treatment plans may later be changed as necessary. To accomplish all this, of course, comprehensive information must be gathered.

As the van deposited me at the clinic I felt hyper-alert, as though I needed to soak in every detail. Entering the clinic through its glass door, I first noticed the warming light. The lobby was open, like an atrium, and sunlight was pouring in. On the back wall, a mural more than two stories tall depicted two simple country women, painted in a style that reminded me of Diego Rivera. They were barefoot, one bending and gathering water from a spring, the other gazing out, both holding terra-cotta water jugs. Dark-haired, they might have been Spanish or Greek, from some other era; they even looked Biblical. The fresco moved me as it connoted healing and simplicity. The overall impression was of freshness and cleanliness. It was a nice, neutral and non-threatening way to introduce patients to the clinic.

An open spiral staircase led to three upper floors. It rose above a little koi pond on the ground floor. The clean, comforting sound of water combined with the lobby's flourishing green plants and trees created a healthy, organic atmosphere. As would be expected of a Swiss clinic, the place was spotless and its efficiency was evident.

The receptionist offered me the standard Schweizerdeutsch morning greeting, "Grutzi," in the ever-lilting tone. Then she handed me a file along with a stern admonition to bring it to each appointment so that the presiding doctor, nurse or practitioner could register notes, prescriptions, treatment, time and date. With a no-nonsense look on her face, she also instructed me never to remove it from the premises. There was nothing fancy about any of it, but I would learn that the system worked well, like a good, dependable Swiss watch.

By 8:00 I was waiting for Dr. Rau outside his second-floor office. When the nurse called me in, I was formally introduced to the doctor, as is the way in Europe, and guided to a chair facing him across his large desk. I scanned the room quickly as I sat. It was lined with old carved panelling, which I suspected he had kept intact from a previous owner. The wood panelling and cabinets gave the space the look of an old European apothecary's shop. Unguents and colored liquids in oddly shaped bottles were ranged in a side room, along with endless narrow drawers holding his homeopathic and isopathic supplies and remedies. A collection of medical books lined another wall. Long horizontal windows on two sides of both of the doctor's rooms allowed the landscape to enter: hills, cows, neat farms in the distance. With the Alps so near, I almost expected to see Heidi walking along the ridge, leading a goat. Large chunks of quartz and amethyst crystals and thriving orchids embellished the space, colorful among the books and files.

I turned my attention to the doctor as we began to talk. Wearing the long white lab coat I learned was his habitual dress, he was much the same as I remembered him: tall and slender, focused and intent. My original impression of him did not change during our appointment. But it was evident this was a slightly different Dr. Rau, not the passionate speaker but Dr. Rau the detective, figuring me out as we talked.

Throughout his work with me, Dr. Rau's choices would be based on several things: the orthodox, conventional medicine of his background; his own observations, as well as those of the other doctors; and his reading of what I needed based on the results of the clinic's testing and Biological Medicine model. As we spoke, our conversation reminded me again and again that this was "whole-istic" medicine, taking emotions and past history into consideration as part of the overall formulation. In this customized medicine one size does not fit all; it regards the individual as a dynamic, ever changing, and unique entity and not just as a set of different organ systems.

In keeping with that approach, the doctor asked a number of questions, rose, and then began looking intently at some x-rays. "Poor Mrs. Horn," he said, pointing at the comprehensive x-rays of my teeth done the day before. "That front tooth with the root canal must come out. It is infected and very old."

Well, the "tooth" moment had arrived, even sooner than I'd thought. Dr. Rau didn't mince words. He looked right at me, his intensity unavoidable, as he explained that he thought the tooth, with its 45-year-old root canal, was infected and dangerous. There was a back tooth with another old root canal that he wanted out also. "The front tooth is on your reproductive organs meridian, the other is on the breast meridian," he explained further. "I have looked at your history. I'm optimistic that your cancer has been environmentally and not genetically caused. I think you can do well, but we must take these steps." He added that while some people have strong enough immune systems to support root canals, those with a comprised immune system, cancer or a history of chemotherapy need to take every precaution.

As he revealed his plan, I confess my back went up. I had avoided dealing with the reality of the tooth extractions I had been warned about. Now, clearly, the time had come when I had to face it.

I already knew, both from my talk with Peter at the dinner table and my earlier reading, that Dr. Rau accepted the meridian system of Traditional Chinese Medicine, using its information as one of the many diagnostic tools in his toolbox. I was familiar with the meridians from acupuncture. The meridian network is seen to comprise twelve main lines of energy, or "qi," running through the body. If the energy flow on a meridian is blocked, the organ system to which it relates as well as a person's overall well-being can be affected. Chinese medicine has been practiced for over 2,500 years. The meridian system is used by the Chinese, Japanese, Koreans, and Tibetans, as well as the many American practitioners of acupuncture, reflexology and shiatsu massage. This was no upstart or unexamined belief system, and I'd had first-hand proof that it worked, always feeling better and more balanced after one of the many acupuncture treatments I'd had over the years. I couldn't really challenge it.

I had not been knowledgeable, though, regarding the connection of the meridian system to teeth. I now learned that each tooth is believed to have an energetic-reflexive connection to a specific meridian, as well as to that meridian's organ system. In simplest terms, if there is a blockage in a tooth, the meridian's energy flow can be impeded. Such blockages could come from several sources, one of the most common being an infected root canal. Dr. Rau never said outright that my front tooth (sitting on the meridian connected with the genitals) caused my cancer, but I believe he thought it made a contribution to this multi-causal disease.

Dr. Rau explained that this old root canal, and by default the front tooth in which it resided, needed to come out to help me regain my health. In the hundreds of cases he has treated, he maintained, almost all of his cancer patients had dental problems: improperly extracted wisdom teeth, cavities, periodontal disease, and root canals. To his mind, all were breeding grounds for bacteria and some were possible sources of mercury poisoning as well.

I was not yet fully ready to accept either the extractions or the principles behind them. But the more he explained, the more I considered the possibility. Since my front tooth had this connection to my reproductive system, my ovaries and uterus, there was certainly a logic behind what he was saying. Besides, nothing in his manner suggested a quack who just loved to remove teeth.

As he talked more, he wrote hurriedly on both a lined, yellow sheet of paper and the file I had been handed that morning. The sheet was the first requisition for the vitamins and drops to be filled at the pharmacy. Dr. Rau said if he could improve the conditions inside my body and strengthen my immune system, he believed there was be a good chance that the cancer would not recur. His optimism helped and encouraged me. It seemed, however, there was a good deal of strengthening that needed to be done. For starters, he prescribed a regime of vitamins and minerals: one all-purpose vitamin, a vitamin C, zinc and selenium. Selenium, a trace element that was new to me, is considered to have properties that may help to prevent cancer. I've been taking it regularly since that first clinic visit.

Every tool Dr. Rau uses is aimed at cleaning out the metaphorical "disease barrel" in order to improve the metabolism and alkalize the milieu (the extra-cellular fluid) as well as to strengthen the gut or intestines, which are often the breeding ground for illness. "The remedies are to rebuild the intestinal flora and your normal internal milieu, to help the body regulate itself," he said as he continued to write and assess.

Naturally, the talk about cancer brought it back to center stage in my mind. At one point, I became tearful. Looking right into my eyes, Dr. Rau spoke firmly. "If you have or have had cancer, you must move away from the fear," he said. "Try to live the day as it comes, look at the birds; this rises up the immune system. And don't go to the Internet to see what more you can do." Viewing cancer as a "breakdown of the self," he said that the patient's perspective must include an open heart. By placing the disease in a less medical, more spiritual context, he helped me relate more easily to what he said. Memories of my summer ruminations in the same vein, helped too, although everything here came as a slightly new slant on things. But I welcomed it all as an explanation of how we would work.

After our conversation, he put me on the examination table and did all the usual MD things, asking me to breathe and cough, examining my skin, doing a little pinch or two on my leg, seemingly to look at skin tone and circulation. He said he would give me a neural therapy shot, an injection of an isopathic remedy to treat the womb area, even though the organ itself was missing.

"Remedy," I learned, can refer to both homeopathic and isopathic preparations. In homeopathy, a key principle is "like cures like"; an intake of something that mimics existing or former symptoms is given to activate and strengthen the immune system. Isopathic formulas, on the other hand, are fabricated according to the principle of "exactly cures exactly." Therefore, different kinds of substances are used in the manufacture. Yet they are comparable in that they are similar in their objectives. Available as both shots and pills, the remedies are designed to promote healing by causing the same or similar symptoms as the disease itself, helping the immune system to fight back, and to strengthen it by doing so. In that sense, they work on some of the same principles as a vaccine.

All fine in theory, I thought—but then I saw the length of the needle he had prepared for me. Thin as it was, I tensed, thinking all of a sudden, "I don't know this person!" There had been plenty of needles in my recent life; I wasn't begging for more. Seeing my expression, Dr. Rau smiled and said it wouldn't hurt. As it slid into my womb area, it didn't hurt at all. My obvious amazement earned another little smile. A brief little pinch was all I felt.

As far as I could tell, no dead bodies were being removed by cover of darkness, so I figured a leap of faith was in order. Besides, it seemed counterproductive to waste his time asking for explanations which I wouldn't have understood anyway. I knew Dr. Rau used remedies and therapies that worked gradually—cumulatively, over a period of time. I presumed this was just the first of many injections.

Although the effects of this one were hard to describe, it felt as if things had opened up, were not so tight. I learned later that he had injected into the "Frankenhauser Space." That sounds a little like a donor's room at the Kennedy Center in Washington, but is actually the soft connective tissue near the cervix. He used a lidocaine product in the remedy. Lidocaine is in the Novocain family and has a relaxing effect. In the USA, an epidural would be a form of this therapy.

Ending our appointment, Dr Rau said it was important to schedule the time at the busy dental clinic as soon as possible. He asked if I would let him know my decision about the teeth fairly quickly. I found I just couldn't say yes right away. It was a shock to think of losing something as visible as my front tooth. It somehow came too close on the heels of having lost other important parts of me.

With my list of things to pick up from the pharmacy, I left his office. At 9:30 I was due at the laboratory for blood tests. The lab did a comprehensive profile—as it turned out, more extensive than the conventional tests I had so often had before. It included some food allergy tests and two tumor marker tests that I recognized from my Yale cancer treatment, as well as other new additions.

At 10:00, I met Dalia Brunner, the charming Brazilian woman who served as the clinic's concierge. She first explained the nuts and bolts of signing up for the bus back and forth to our lodgings—important, as those who forgot to sign up could be left behind. I learned that Hans, the bus driver, was like a Swiss watch. If the clock said 10:00 and he was supposed to be elsewhere at 10:05, he would leave for elsewhere. She also reminded me of the importance of leaving my file whenever I left the clinic, told me where to make telephone calls and get lunch, and encouraged me to ask anything I wanted about treatments.

While the logistics of the clinic had that ubiquitous Swiss crispness, my discussions with Dalia reminded me that it was also flexible on many "bigger picture" items. If I heard of something not on program and wished to try it, I was free to do so. If I wanted to cancel a second treatment of something I hadn't enjoyed, as long as it was not considered vital, I was similarly free. This flexibility reminded me of the clinic's whole-person approach. From the perspective of this kind of medicine, forcing a patient to do something that felt wrong would be counterproductive at best. Being able to make changes and having choices helps the patient engage in the process. It also demonstrates trust in the wisdom of the patient's own intuition to have a sense of what feels right.

Dalia gave me various documents, including a sheet of paper on which to list my remedies or diet supplements. It had different blank spaces in which I would indicate when, how often, at what time, and for how long I was to take each, as well as whether or not it could be mixed with other medications. This was a helpful—indeed, essential—organizing tool, since the number and kinds of supplements would quickly begin to add up.

My last appointment before lunch was with Dr. Seiler, the gynecologist. He was a taciturn man who performed thorough pelvic and breast exams almost wordlessly. After my experience at Yale, such exams and their sonograms left me slightly on tenterhooks. Happily, he pronounced me clean and clear. He saw nothing suspicious, he said. My breasts and ovarian area seemed in good health. The Polaroid-size sonogram images were attached to my file, already growing noticeably in thickness. With the exam done, Dr. Seiler grew more talkative, giving me a brief description of his time studying in the States and telling how much he enjoyed his stay there.

It had been a busy morning. I was grateful that clinic scheduling always allowed a break for lunch, even if the time had to be cut back due to an appointment. In addition to cooking for the Schutzi, Irene was also the chef of the luncheon restaurant adjacent to the clinic, ensuring that we all ate well throughout our respective stays. The Winkelstein Restaurant seems somehow part of the clinic, only a five minutes' walk away. But the clinic didn't own it and outsiders could eat there, too.

Entering, I saw a buffet table practically groaning with the freshest of salad ingredients: seeds and nuts, several lettuces, sprouts, and bowls of grated carrots, zucchini, and Japanese daikon. A vegetable soup also was on tap. The hot buffet offered a tofu dish, another with quinoa and vegetables, and a third with animal protein, which was chicken that day. Vinegars, herbal condiments and a variety of oils, from olive and flax to sunflower, were available for dressings. There was fresh bread, tea, and water, as always without ice. No dairy was anywhere in sight, but there was a machine that brewed espresso and decaf coffee. There were even some cookies to be had.

One of the acquaintances I had made the day before was already at the restaurant when I appeared. A new arrival like me, Gail Miller had been treated without surgery, chemotherapy or radiation for Stage 4 breast cancer. My first sight of Gail—swathed in fur and gold jewelry, carrying what I learned was her ubiquitous Vuitton bag and sporting a deep suntan—had not been positive. I had wrongly tagged her as some spoiled Palm Beach beauty. That couldn't have been further from who she really was: one of the most down-to-earth, bright and darling people I ever knew. The fur was on loan from her mother-in-law and dated from the 1930s. (Someone had managed to find cold storage on the island of Kauai, where she lived.) When we started to chat the morning before, we had bonded almost instantly. At lunch we had more time to talk, and began to form a friendship that lasted until the very end.

As we ate and chatted, I discovered that Gail was knowledgeable about several of the clinic's modalities, including thermography. This diagnostic tool was also available in the States, used most commonly in California, where Gail had found one of the acknowledged experts in its use.

She had a son she adored, a successful design business on Kauai, and a marriage about which she was non-comittal. Her mother-in-law had accompanied her to Switzerland and was having a wellness treatment. Gail did not believe in chemotherapy, but she was very well read about all cancer treatments, both conventional and alternative. Although we were very different, we meshed easily together. I think I sensed even at that first lunch that she would become the most important friend I would meet during that stay.

At 2:00, lunch finished, I showed up for the far infrared sauna. The printout I was handed noted that it utilized infrared instead of regular heat. Infrared heat waves were developed by NASA and reach the body directly, without heating the air inside the sauna as a Swedish sauna does. Users can therefore breathe more comfortably, and the atmosphere inside the sauna is more pleasant. This heat reaches more deeply into the tissues than a regular sauna, making it efficacious in removing heavy metals, such as mercury, from the tissues. Far infrared sauna was, and is, an important tool at the clinic because it is considered a good detoxification mechanism, an immune booster, and a possible suppressor of cancer cells.

The heat was indeed very pleasant—not as scorching as a regular sauna. There was no need to jump into a freezing shower to cool off before going back in for more. The timer was set at thirty-five minutes. When the timer "binged," I had established the kind of good sweat the clinic wanted which had been difficult for me to attain in the past. Feeling warm, I dressed and hustled off to the mysterious HRI, wondering if I would have this many appointments every day. I decided, wrongly, that these first days would be busier than later ones because there were so many initial diagnostic tests to perform. I soon discovered that each day would be packed.

The mysterious HRI turned out to be the Heart Rate Variability diagnostic, a computerized testing of the pulse rate at various stages of physical effort. The test looks at the two principle parts of the autonomic nervous system, the parasympathetic and the sympathetic systems, in which Dr. Rau believes there should be what he calls a subtle balance.

In simplest terms, the autonomic nervous system is mostly involuntary, regulating heartbeat, blood pressure, eye muscle activity, peristalsis and all the activities our body performs automatically throughout the day and night. The parasympathetic component controls our "rest and digest" mode, while the sympathetic one gears up "fight or flight" responses. The information in my clinic packet noted that imbalance in the autonomic nervous system is very often a "precursor to chronic disease, or even cancer." My doctors would hypothesize that because of traumas growing up, I had lived on high alert, in sympathetic mode, for a long time. That was partly responsible, in their view, for wearing down my immune system.

I was adorned with a black rubber belt on my upper midriff and a computerized "pulse writer" that recorded my pulse before, during, and after a slight physical exertion. The variations of the heart rhythm measured "reaction capability." A low reaction capability could indicate chronic stress, fatigue, and even chronic degenerative illnesses. My reaction capability was low during this first visit, leading Dr. Rau to tell me later than my heart was under stress. Later, I discovered research revealing that chemo may weaken the heart muscle, though the effect may not be evident until long after treatment.

With the HRI testing finished, my first full day at the clinic ended. Only when waiting for Hans and the van to take me back to the Schutzi did I realize I hadn't signed up. It was two minutes past departure time. Just as Dalia had warned he had gone, Swiss watch style. I walked back to the Schutzi, the walk a good antidote to all the thoughts bouncing around in my head.

It had been a great day: interesting, stimulating and educational. The nurses had been caring, with no sign of acrylic finger nails or negative attitudes. Though some of the tests and treatments were surprising, with the exception of the potential tooth extractions I had no problem accepting them. My new friend Gail was a find. As I walked, it made me laugh to think how many times I had initially not liked someone only to become good friends with them later. We seemed to bond instantly, but maybe that's because people confronted with mortality tend to react more quickly, knowing there could be less time to waste in delay or procrastination.

At dinner that night I once more sat at the big table. Peter Lieberson was again sitting next to me. We had another talk about teeth. He was sympathetic about my conversation with Dr. Rau, as well as the resistance I felt towards extractions. But he'd had a couple of teeth removed, so he supported the idea, saying it would be better for me to get rid of root canals. I listened carefully, but my bed was calling. It had been a long, full day. I fell asleep almost immediately after rigging my overcoat over the duvet, tucking it in on one side, and hoping it would *stay* there and keep my feet warm.

My journal tells me I awoke on Wednesday feeling refreshed. My energy level was a bit calmer and I was greatly anticipating the day. As I meditated, the Dalai Lama's face appeared with an expression of forgiveness and deep sweetness. For a long time, I had known that forgiveness would be an essential part of my master plan for moving forward. There was a lot to forgive, especially in myself. I wondered if the clinic's remedies were starting to work already. Could one day erase resistance, or at least open me up a bit, so more air was let in and new thinking was free to emerge? I hoped so, I really hoped so.

13

Erstaunlich*

Madness may not be all breakdown, it may be
breakthrough.

— R.D Laing

I had survived and even enjoyed my first three days at Paracelsus,
intrigued with all there was to learn and fascinated by the clinic itself.
Friday brought the first of the three hyperthermia sessions on my
schedule. On the evidence, I can say that I survived it. Enjoyment was
another matter entirely but it was a unique experience.

Full-body heat treatments are one of the most important treatments at Paracelsus. Hyperthermia is designed to kill cancer cells
which, apparently, do not like heat. It also strengthens the immune
system and encourages the elimination of toxins residing in the tissues. As Dr. Rau describes it, "Whole body hyperthermia is intensely
effective in stimulating the immune system. It increases metabolic
function and white blood cell capacity," white cells being the body's
defense against infectious diseases and other invaders. According to
some German research, with each rise of one degree centigrade in
body temperature, the metabolic rate increases 100%, with benefits
lasting for about two weeks.

---

*German for astounding, amazing

The research materials don't dwell on the possibility of emotional release due to the intense heat—but I can now talk about that at length.

My first hyperthermia began with undressing, choosing music, putting on a surgical gown and then attaching a lot of gear. I was set up with an IV drip, a rectal thermometer, and a heart monitor clipped to my ear. My veins are small, so it's never easy to get the intravenous drip attached. That day was no exception. Once attached, the IV was taped securely onto my arm, for stability or maybe to prevent me conducting the Symphony *Pathetique.* The materials I was given describe the intravenous drip's contents as something Dr. Rau pioneered to "turn the patient's metabolism to alkalinity and into an anti-oxidative stage. In it is a combination of high-dose vitamins and immune-boosting alkaline infusions."

I lay down on the terrycloth-covered bed. Around it, rectangles of lined, silvery fabric hung from a rigid frame. Velcro closures joined, they formed a rectangular tent. Though the top had a small window opening, once the Velcro was pressed into place, I was totally and claustrophobically enclosed, surrounded by the light and warmth of the infrared heat sources lining the inside. A nurse would be there the entire time to watch my progress. A doctor monitored the treatment, not in continuous attendance, but coming in periodically when all was well and available immediately if any emergency arose. If I became anxious, the nurse assured me, oxygen would be available to ease my breathing.

These precautions were necessary. The goal was for my body to reach around 103 degrees over the course of the treatment, so the patient must be carefully watched. Fever was the objective, sweat being seen as the conduit for a cleansing detoxification as well as for all the other benefits. Such high temperatures are safe for short periods, but anything higher or longer can be dangerous.

I didn't know what to expect, except that it would be hot. I was told that the temperature would rise gradually; when the desired temperature had been reached, the lights would go off. Perspiration would increase as the temperature rose, so I was forewarned that my robe would be soaked at the end. I was girlishly proud that I didn't perspire very much, not yet knowing that sweat is one of the body's best regulatory mechanisms, essential for removing toxins. My new friend Gail had said her experience of hyperthermia had been pleasant. A lover of sun and heat anyway, she had simply dropped off to sleep.

My experience was quite different. As the temperature gradually rose the New Age CD I had selected started to play surf and whale sounds. I lay there thinking it wasn't so bad, reflecting on all that had happened since Sunday. The lights were bright but the heat was manageable and, at first, relaxing. Then suddenly a wave surged up inside me, a feeling almost like vomiting but not localized to any one place in my body.

Still higher heat caused me to lose any ability to stay in control, to keep the metaphorical lid on. Feeling upset and threatened, I began thrashing about, causing some pain in my needle arm. I tried to stay still, not wanting to displace the IV drip. This was the strangest thing I have ever experienced. One part of me knew who and where I was—for example, I could control the arm with the needle. The other part of me was experiencing such strong volcanic emotion that it felt entirely different, as if there were two of me.

Even as it was happening, I knew I had no power to control my emotions. I couldn't stop myself from moaning and crying. I felt suddenly terrified that my father was hurting me again. These feelings are hard to describe. I only knew that a strong fear of my father was driving me, even while my rational self knew I was safe. I had no images of the locker room—it was my body talking, not my mind.

As the intense heat melted my control, the effects of trauma that I had hidden, held and buried for decades were released in a startling and powerful way. It was like an inner tornado had arrived out of nowhere. My mind couldn't control the pressure or the emotional pain my body released. I screamed for help.

Hearing me, the nurse called Dr. Rau's office. He and another doctor appeared quickly. They asked me to describe my feelings, but I was sobbing, frightened and inconsolable. I was talked through a breathing exercise while Dr. Rau gave me some foot reflexology, both of which calmed me down somewhat.

As the two doctors discussed the best way to respond to my distress, a point of disagreement arose between them. Dr. Rau, who prefers moving toward the future rather than the past, thought the conversation should move in a forward direction. The other physician believed that the hyperthermia had tapped into old grief and fears never fully expressed, and that the better solution was letting it all out.

By then, thanks to the breathing, talking, and massage plus the reassuring, compassionate presence of the doctors, the worst was over. In any case the heat would now start to decline, having reached the desired level. So the hyperthermia continued. It was not easy. It was still hot, and I couldn't stop myself from whimpering like a hurt animal. The emotional storm had subsided but I wasn't completely settled. A couple of other eruptions came later, each less intense than the earlier one. By the end of the treatment I was exhausted. Finally, the heaters were extinguished. As the various tubes and the IV needle were removed, I lay in a pool of sweat, the towels wrapping me thoroughly soaked.

Physically and emotionally a wreck, I couldn't get up on my own. When I asked for assistance, the nurse brought in a little stool with wheels. Sitting on that, I was rolled to another room. There I lay on a massage table, covered with a light blanket, to cool down and rest for several minutes. Seeing how pale and low in energy I was, the attending doctor offered to drive me back to the Schutzi. There, I went upstairs to lie in a cool bathtub for some time before descending down to dinner.

I slept well that night. I remember waking in the middle of the night and feeling well—cleansed, somehow, almost as if I'd gotten over a virus or a bout of the flu. I felt calm, not hyper, and ready to move forward.

The next day I received so many sympathetic looks from fellow patients, nurses and staff that I knew I'd been heard throughout the building. I was embarrassed until I learned that my responses were really what they hope for in a patient. When I win the lottery, the Paracelsus hyperthermia rooms will be soundproofed, with a plaque near the bed testifying to the beauty inherent in letting go for good.

When I later gave Gail a description of my hyperthermia, she helped, as always. She nicknamed me "Breakthrough," knowing even before I did that there had been big benefits from the difficult experience. Over time, I felt those benefits as well. Pandora's Box had been flung wide open. Middle-aged demons held within me for decades, had been summoned and evicted, leaving me purged and relieved.

The full days at the clinic continued. Over the weekend, I was given a new "job": grappling with mistletoe injections. Mistletoe is an important cancer drug in Europe, especially in the German-speaking countries and the Netherlands, where it is used as a palliative medicine rather than a cure. It was first proposed as a treatment in 1920 by Rudolph Steiner, whom I've mentioned before. Among other things, the founder of anthroposophic medicine, biodynamic organic farming and eurythmy, Steiner believed that the human body was organized by certain forces. Some of them, the "higher organizing forces," control and organize cell growth, forming the tissues and organs. Steiner believed that these forces were deficient in cancer patients, writing that cancer formed "when regulation of both the body's physical and spiritual defenses faltered." His ideas are complex and well outside the medical mainstream. His prolific but complicated writing is difficult to comprehend as well. As I understand his beliefs, he held that without a strong spiritual dimension, a person's health would break down. Something extra, he felt, kept us alive, something other than our heart and brain. Mistletoe could assist in re-establishing a regulatory balance, and thus fight back against tumors.

Back at that December seminar in Massachusetts, Dr. Steven Johnson had explained why. He had commented that "mistletoe can bring degenerative cells back into a bioactive state if given correctly. It acts as an immune regulator, not a stimulator. The better it is administered, the better it works." Mistletoe lectin is now being studied as a treatment for cancer, although in 2009, Memorial Sloan-Kettering announced it could find nothing measurable to show that it had merit as a cure.

I had no arguments with mistletoe, but anyone who cares to check with my daughters will discover I am a real chicken. I hate the sight of blood, dislike needles, and used to be fairly useless to anyone needing nursing. Picking up my mistletoe at the pharmacy, I expected the pharmacist to look at me sympathetically. Instead, she just handed me the boxes, inquiring matter-of-factly, "Did you want the long or the short needles?" My eyes widened. Though longing to say "I don't want them at all," I obediently signed the receipt—taking the short needles, of course.

Dr. Rau had demonstrated how to pinch the skin and inject quickly. It hadn't hurt when he had done it. The mistletoe wasn't injected into a vein, so the mechanics of loading the needle weren't so critical. Nonetheless, I toyed with the needles and ampoules most of the weekend, taking one or the other out of the box, then putting it back, postponing. Finally Gail, who'd self-injected homeopathic shots for a long time, got me started. Giving me some courage, she showed me again how to do it. At first, watching the skin break with a kind of "pop" and then bleeding was moderately upsetting. But I have to admit that it's an uncomplicated procedure, one I got used to fairly quickly after Gail's tuition. Again, I was participating in my own healing process and being positively challenged. On my walks around Lustmuhle, I now noticed mistletoe balls growing in the trees, something I hadn't noticed before.

Administering mistletoe shots was something which I would do for over a year. Like many of the clinic's treatments, it works gradually. My new schedule of swallowing remedies and supplements was just the same. The vitamins, mineral supplements, algae tablets, and digestive enzymes, as well as the mistletoe needles and ampoules, had begun to take over the small brown dresser in my room. I viewed them as symbols pointing to a better future, especially as I was feeling so upbeat in just those few days. Not least of all, I felt calmer and more relaxed, and my curiosity was increasing with each treatment.

14

Reinventing the Wheel

My final word before I'm done, is 'Cancer can be rather fun.'

—J.B.S. Haldane

Gail and I spent time together over the weekend, walking the hills, talking about the treatments and sharing more about our lives. Among other things, I learned about her deeply committed Christian faith. My next conversation with Dr. Rau would come on Monday and, for the most part, I was looking forward to it. There was a lot more to learn about this new idea of health in which I was engaged and which was already producing good results. No other doctors had ever spoken to me of either the emotional side of illness as an elemental part of healing, or of the impact and importance of cells in their individuality.

I woke Monday feeling something like an old hand, having already experienced most of the treatments that I would have over the next two weeks. Sitting outside Dr. Rau's office, flipping through out-of-date German magazines or the occasional dog-eared copy of *The New Yorker* magazine, I was enthusiastic—almost. Another neural therapy was probably in the cards, along with a further expansion of the supplement list. But none of that bothered me. Somehow, I had arrived in another zone, bringing to it a less nervous kind of energy, one that both gave me strength and increased my hopefulness.

I knew the dental decision would be next. Because I'd kept the doctor waiting for my answer about the extractions, I was slightly nervous. And there would be the issue of hyperthermia to discuss as well.

Once I was in his office, Dr. Rau brought up the hyperthermia right away. I told him I was better, but with a knowing smile, he said he knew it had been difficult. He had heard I was exhausted afterwards, and hoped I'd had a restful weekend. In his reassuring way, he reiterated that all the clinic's treatments worked together synergistically, and that over time "the patient becomes more dynamic, and begins to feel more whole and integrated." Looking at me quite seriously, he told me what a good reaction I had had to the heat, with just the kind of response they hoped for. "In the situation of a high fever, patients begin to have fantasies," he wrote in a magazine article I later read, likening them to a child's hallucinations during fever. "The same thing happens in cancer patients and it is very interesting. What comes into their minds are very often key experiences of their lives. We talk with the patient, so the patient can explore what emerges. Then we help them work through it afterwards. Patients like the hyperthermia, even though it is difficult and uncomfortable to get through; they feel successful when they come through this psychological clearing. It is often very mind-opening." That was exactly what I experienced. Today, I attribute a good part of my overall improvements to the hyperthermia treatments.

Dr. Rau said that neither my mind nor my body had been capable of dealing with my childhood sexual trauma. I was simply too young to have been able to process the event. My father's death two years later, right as I hit puberty, had been a second blow. Suppression had been the only solution. But those successive traumas had been a strain both on my immune and autonomic nervous systems. From then on, in his opinion, I had tended to remain stuck in the "fight or flight" response, which made it difficult to really relax and helped produce those frequent, terrible nightmares.

Of course, the issue of the teeth arose. Resistant as I had been, the reason for the extractions had become clearer to me. Rather than seeing the teeth as orthodox doctors do, in isolation, Dr. Rau's belief was that even if you sealed the tooth with a root canal, it remained connected to the lymph system, a crucial part of the body's regulatory mechanism. No matter how skillfully the procedure was executed, it could spill out bacteria and block blood and energy flow.

I gave him the go-ahead for the extractions and he was visibly pleased. He immediately instructed his secretary to call the dental clinic regarding appointment availability, also requesting a replacement dental plate, sometimes called a "flipper." More supplements were prescribed, and I received another neural therapy shot. This time it was two short jabs into the tonsils, which the clinic believes can cause problems in those of us that still retain them.

After that appointment, I headed for the Dark Field Microscopy room. The dark field test examines a drop of blood taken from the finger with a simple pinprick, enabling the technician to see bacteria, a virus or fungus: the three important stages, or "valences" as the clinic called them, which lead to the development of chronic conditions and illnesses. A tiny Sleeping Beauty prick to my finger saw a drop pop out, which was captured and rubbed onto two or three glass slides. The slides were placed under the dark field microscope, so called because the background is almost black. They first provided a view of my body's inner terrain, showing the functioning of the live blood cells; they were then studied further to see how they broke down over time. The examination placed the cells under stress by depriving them of oxygen to observe how they (and other entities in the cellular fluid) reacted. In addition to bacteria, viruses and fungi, the clinician looked for endobionts (tiny microbes of plant origin, which may evolve into a form that can cause disease) and plasma. This view of living blood could detect degenerative tendencies, gave a snapshot of the internal milieu, and reveal both current and upcoming developments. The small, white-painted test room held a gallery of dark-field pictures of different cellular situations. Even I could tell some of them didn't look so good.

My own blood was displayed on a monitor about 20 inches wide. I could see my cells dancing around as the microscope slowly focused, an amazing sight. Dr. Rau came in, looking at the projected slides and discussed what he saw with the clinician. Even though the conversation was in German, I could pick up a few words. Clearly, there would be more remedies coming down the pike.

Dr Rau explained the testing and its purposes. One focus was to determine whether my cells were sticking together in what are called "rouleaux"—not a healthy thing—or flowing easily through the cellular fluid as they should. They also looked to see if too much light was coming through the cells. A "central glimmer" would mean that the cell wall was too thin, suggesting a problem with fatty acids. "Shadow cells," which have lost their cell walls, might be old cells leaving. Apparently they are a sign of healing, indicating that weak cells are being replaced. A circle inside a cell with a big dot in the center could be evidence of protein overload. White cells "herding" in clusters meant that the immune system is excited about something, good or bad; I was told that herding was different from *rouleaux*, which were made of cells piled on top of each other. The amount of information the clinic could glean from these pictures was fascinating. Why, I wondered, did doctors in the States not use this system?

At the end of the day, I was stopped at the door by one of the receptionists. She handed me a revised schedule indicating several dental appointments, all underlined in light blue highlighter. I smiled, but a slight groan went through my newly energized body. All of my other appointments—two more hyperthermias, infusions, ozone therapy, colonics, indiba (local hyperthermia to produce small fevers in the cells), saunas and my favorite, reflexology—had been rearranged around the dentistry.

Of course, I also had to stop at the pharmacy. Managing the myriad of drops, capsules, tablets and injections, each to be taken at specific times, had become a mini-career. Success demanded diligence, commitment and organization, plus a large pill box. Going out to lunch or dinner, I had to take any necessary supplements with me.

An hour before dinner, I downed a snappy little red pill. Called Wobenzym, it is a combination of enzymes, including both pineapple and papaya derivatives and antioxidants. It's intended to strengthen the immune, cardiovascular and nervous systems as well as maintain optimal hormonal balance in the body. When I returned to the U.S., I would be surprised to learn that Wobenzym is popular in the United States, as well as being one of most successful enzyme products sold in Germany.

Dr. Rau had also prescribed special immune booster drops intended to help the intestinal tract, adding to two other sets of homeopathic drops, one to remove toxins from kidney cells, another to detox and stimulate the lymph vessels. The large intestine is the body's largest excretory organ for waste products and toxins; the clinic held that it sometimes needed stimulation to avoid re-toxifying the body through the intestinal walls. Though the variety of treatments sometimes obscured this to lay eyes, I was beginning to realize how well–thought-out the clinic's program was, every aspect carefully examined and addressed.

What I was *not* given were any antibiotics. Except in the most urgent cases they were regarded as an enemy at Paracelsus, or at least a false friend. They are designed to make symptoms disappear quickly—but symptoms provide clues to solving the mystery of illness, and to obliterate them can leave that trail cold. The goal at Paracelsus was ultimately to relieve symptoms naturally, by discovering root causes, improving the body's own healing capacity, and letting it take over in the quest to regain health.

When my blood work came back, it showed high mercury levels among other things. Not so high, however, as another American patient who had played with mercury from thermometers as a kid, watching it roll around the floor, and later had been a chemistry teacher. His mercury count was in the stratosphere, he had lost much of the nerve and muscle coordination in his hands, and he had come to the clinic out of desperation. He stayed for many weeks more than I did, and mentioned to me that he was feeling better. It seems mercury is difficult to get out of the tissues, however, so the clinic uses a number of treatments intended to help the body release it.

One of them, the far infrared sauna, I had already experienced and enjoyed. Now, the mercury in my old fillings was carefully removed. It was done with a tiny vacuum to ensure that I ingested no mercury. There was some grinding, probing and scraping, too. At least, I thought, the mercury was out—from my teeth, if not yet from my tissues. My blood work confirmed that there was work to be done on this front.

Mercury has long been known to be damaging to human health; it is a powerful neurotoxin. The expression "mad as a hatter" refers to the symptoms hat-makers developed as a result of mercury exposure: erratic behavior, excessive drooling, tremors, numbness, and other disabilities. Until men stopped wearing hats, Danbury, Connecticut, was the center of the hat-making industry in the United States and had its own special reputation for madness; tremors were called the "Danbury shakes." The list of other symptoms of mercury poisoning is long and painful and includes organ damage and the possibility of heart disease. I came to question why anything that by American law must go into a hazmat container was still allowed to be deliberately placed in our heads in the form of amalgam fillings. The knowledge of mercury I gained also put me off tuna and other large fish, which have higher mercury content than smaller ones.

Mercury is still used in amalgam dental fillings to bind the silver, copper, zinc, and tin into an alloy. Although amalgam fillings are a controversial issue, the American Dental Association has not prohibited their general use, saying the mercury is not harmful when it binds to the other metals. More progressive dentists today avoid it, pointing out that amalgam packaging warns of the hazards of mercury. It melts at temperatures above 95 degrees Fahrenheit, thus potentially releasing toxic material from amalgam fillings which are not far from the brain.

Until my stay at the clinic, I had never considered that drinking hot beverages, grinding my teeth, and even chewing could cause mercury to seep into my body. The body might tolerate the seepage for years, I learned, but eventually it would take its toll. Dr. Rau says the body's compensatory mechanism ultimately goes haywire, swinging wildly out of balance. Because mercury suppresses the pituitary gland, which controls the functions of the other endocrine glands, the removal of this neurotoxin is considered very important. In addition to having the fillings removed and undergoing the far infrared saunas, I was prescribed algae and spirulina (another green single-celled algae) which bind with mercury and help in its excretion.

I accepted everything: infusions, treatments, supplements and shots. It wasn't hard, for the most part. I found the clinic's unique combination of elements such as homeopathy, Traditional Chinese Medicine and Ayurvedic medicine, as well as newer diagnostic techniques combined with allopathic medicine, not only unique but inspiring. Facing the dental work had been the most difficult barrier to overcome. Now, having surrendered to it, I let those helpful twins, intuition and my old trust in Switzerland, take over. My faith in human nature had been rebuilt long ago in this country, my expectations of fair behavior met rather than dashed as they had been back home. I trusted the Swiss, and I had hope. The doors to change had opened, at least at this moment, right here, in this medicine, at this clinic, in this canton of Switzerland.

15

The Birth of the Death of the Past

Will wonders never cease?

— DAVID GARRICK, 18TH CENTURY ACTOR

The clinic usually bustled, with something of a campus atmosphere about it. Doctors and nurses chatted to each other and patients would rush from one appointment to the next throughout the morning and again in the afternoon after the lunch break. On one floor, a tray of many different teas was on offer, each in aid of some part of the body—an organ system, the blood or the liver. Each day, I noticed touches which supported my growing impression of an innovative and thoughtful organization doing work it loved to do.

As I went to my various appointments, I was always on the lookout for Gail. Having abandoned the expensive hotel in town, she was now ensconced with her mother-in-law in an apartment at the tiny Hotel Vadian on a side street in St. Gallen, only minutes away from the clinic on the red train. Her old-fashioned Scottish thrift was perpetually shining out from her stylish Louis Vuitton wallet. She invited me to stay a couple of nights in this tiny apartment, and we deepened our friendship, shared some secrets, and drank a forbidden thimbleful of red wine—bad for the detox, but great for the soul.

Having mercury vacuumed out of my teeth was a piece of cake (the only cake allowed) compared to the second hyperthermia that soon followed. Slightly uncomfortable, even embarrassed, about all the noise I'd manufactured during the first one, I made a tentative climb up the stairs. I didn't know what to expect this time, but I feared it would be upsetting yet again. Part of me wished I didn't have to be there. Still, I had been so moved by the emotional catharsis I'd experienced that I'd made no attempt to cancel this second appointment. So there I was, on the second Tuesday of my stay, undressing as obediently as before.

A different nurse was on duty that day. Rita was one of the veterans, a small woman with big blue eyes and a caring nature. She became Mutter (Mother) Rita, to me about halfway through the session: looking after me, handing me cold drinks and compresses through the little window carved into the top of my enclosure, encouraging me as my temperature rose. That happened more quickly this time, she said, referring to the notes and adding, "Gut, gut." I too felt everything was going well until the end, when my parents paid me a visit.

They appeared behind me, standing side by side, crying and oddly miniaturized. I wondered which guardian angel had made them so small and saw Billy Burke, smiling and dressed as good witch Glinda from *The Wizard of Oz*, holding up her wand. I started to laugh. But suddenly a more powerful physical reaction overcame me. My heart, stomach, pelvis and genitals—all of them were intensely releasing emotion from the cells themselves, letting go of more stored grief, humiliation and pain. I was sweating profusely, something I had never done before. It was amazing there was so much left to let go of.

As he had during my first hyperthermia, the attending doctor hurried briskly in to ask what was happening. When I told him who my visitors were, he had an idea. "Why not get rid of them for once and for all, so they can't get at you? Where do you want to put them?"

It was a great suggestion. Empowered, I responded. "In front of me, so I can watch them and see what they are doing. I don't want them at my back." I told my mother to leave, saying goodbye, telling her "deal with your own problems and baggage." Addressing my father, I said something like, "You gave me the gift of life and then you crushed me. Go." Cowering, full of grief, they disappeared.

Again the hyperthermia, though taxing, had produced a hugely dramatic but thoroughly beneficial encounter. One of the doctors suggested for a long time that, "the way I experienced the most important things was as the little girl in me," leaving me stuck with "the bad experiences that happened back then." If I could understand and internalize that, I could try to substitute more positive thoughts, perhaps telling myself I was leaving behind the cancer and its possible causes." This time my parents didn't loom large, they were small, powerless, and obedient to my direction. With the doctor's help, I had gained the ability to decide the outcome of our encounters. Hopefully, in leaving the terror of the past behind for good, I was strengthening my capacity to leave cancer behind as well. Afterwards, I was again exhausted at both the physical and emotional levels. But I recognized a clarity and cleanliness, as if something was over.

Back at the hotel at the end of the day, I wrote, "Momentous. I gave birth to the death of the past. How do I build on Friday's experience? How do I keep it up?"

Now at the halfway mark of my time at Paracelsus, I was beginning to understand what had been a mystery. Dr. Rau's prescription to his patients is to have "joy, faith and trust." Easy for him to say, I had thought at first, but not always easy for patients to do given how many of us had cancer or other very serious illness. But slowly, I was coming to see that he was right. I was still walking around, so there was much to be thankful for. Constant obsession and worry did nothing but increase stress. "Live the day as it comes," the doctor also advised, and "make cancer your friend. You got it for a reason." Getting cancer "for a reason" struck a major chord. Getting a handle on that reason was my assignment: one that had already directed me to the past, without me really having realized it.

As part of the doctor's prescription to enjoy each day, I savored the pleasures of Switzerland. On the middle weekend of my stay, Gail, her mother-in-law and I went by train to see the lake near Constance. The *Bodensee* is a natural gem of sparkling water with a coastline in three countries, Switzerland, Austria, and Germany. Photos from the nineteenth century show white steamers cruising gently along the lake, smoke curling softly around their smokestacks. The twenty-first century offers a more heterogeneous scene. Though less romantic to a critical eye, more *Sleepless in Seattle* than *Last Year at Marienbad*, it is still beautiful.

Having seen the sights, we returned to Gail's temporary apartment in St. Gallen, the birthplace of Paracelsus himself. Gail was a modern-day alchemist: the meals emerging from her sad excuse for a kitchen never failed to astound. From one small pot barely large enough to boil a single egg, she prepared feasts of beans, lentils, onions and carrots, all organic to the *nth* degree, dripping in cold pressed olive oil, garlic chopped into everything, all sprinkled with Dr. Rau's Himalayan salt with its special minerals. We were munching our way into alkalinity and good health, but it was also delicious.

I needed all that nourishment. Monday would be D-Day, Dentist Day, when I would join the club I came to call the PWMT, People with Missing Teeth.

That Monday, not without apprehension, I headed to the dental facility. Above the entrance there was a stained glass window of Paracelsus, the presiding spirit and alchemist. Beyond that one historic touch, the dental offices were completely modern, full of art and plants, with spacious treatment rooms and corridors. The picturesque views, some looking out on Santis Mountain and its range, were not enough to quiet my apprehension. Nor was the fact that the dentist was an attractive man with a buzz cut who looked quite efficient.

The front tooth didn't come out without a fight. But as it finally released, I experienced a sort of electrical charge, almost an epiphany. In that split second, I knew this had been a good decision. My back right molar, the one on the breast meridian was removed as well. Drops were handed to me, but I had no problem with either wound healing or pain. I even had dinner that night, chewing in the ways of a contortionist. The extractions would need several days to heal before I received the flipper, a Bazooka-Bubble-Gum-pink plastic-and-metal device contoured to my mouth that would cover my upper palate. I hated the idea of covering the roof of my mouth but I hated more the idea of no front tooth.

The day after the extractions, I had my first appointment with Wolfgang Haas. I had noticed his powerful, energetic presence from the very beginning of my stay. Striding purposefully, he was always immaculate in white duck pants and a white tee-shirt. He looked a bit like Paul Newman, but with close-cropped salt-and-pepper hair and the profile of a Roman emperor. He hadn't been booked for me originally, but a patient acquaintance had said that he was amazing, so I asked if he could be fitted in to my schedule, and the clinic had made the changes.

Mr. Haas was a revelation. Although he resists any packaging or labeling of his work, when pressed he describes it as manual therapy, kinesiology and personal counseling. Essentially, he was a healer with a huge toolbox. Like all of those at the clinic, he believed that "outside pressures and emotional strains led to manifestations in the body." On the clinic printouts that described each treatment or practitioner, he had written that "the body remembers its past. With my treatments, I accompany the body through the process of re-finding, or approaching as closely as possible to, the person's elementary, relaxed and unrestrained state of former being."

Using kinesiology, the movement of the muscles, Mr. Haas determined where energy was blocked, then employed both talk and touch to find the reasons for the blockage. All this happens over an hour's time as the participant lies on a massage table, fully clothed.

Our work together resulted in some fascinating insights and breakthroughs, each session accompanied by either a physical or emotional release, and often, a welling up of tears and emotion. Our first session "marked the beginnings of a permanent change," I wrote in my diary. As he questioned me, he used my arm for muscle testing, almost as if it were a polygraph needle. (Applied kinesilogy has become more and more widely used here in the States as well.) I was open about my father, my anger, my pain and sorrow, and what I perceived as my father's guilt. I explained the actual event as I remembered it and described the atmosphere of "spiritual incest" in the household. I left the session drained, but also released and relaxed.

In a subsequent session, another remarkable experience took me by surprise, moving me to tears and astonishment. For some reason I can't explain—except to say that it came from a deep place—I blurted out to Mr. Haas that I felt guilt about a death of someone I had never met, my Uncle Billy. Billy, my grandmother Jeanne's favorite, was a handsome soldier who drowned in a shallow swimming pool just before he left for the war in Europe. I had never consciously thought about him, although he had popped up periodically in family conversations. It turned out I somehow felt responsible, not for his death, but for my grandmother's unhappiness after this great loss.

Mr. Haas asked me to imagine my grandmother being in the room. I brought Grandma Jeanne up in my mind, still in the old pink quilted dressing gown I remembered so well. He asked if I'd like to bring Billy in, suggesting that I place him where I felt he should be. Agreeing, I imagined them together by the small porcelain sink located about four feet away from me in the treatment room. Suddenly, they put their arms around each other. As I saw my grandmother's smiling face, happy and at peace, reunited with her beloved son, tears of gratitude poured down my own face. Where this all came from, I haven't a clue. But dealing with it did something for me, released some old burden that I'd felt but never understood.

Not all of our work concerned the past. Dr. Haas, who grew to know me as our sessions went on, had useful insights into my future. He suggested that the man I choose to be with when I was ready again be someone "strong in the ways men are thought of as strong." He saw me as having archetypally female strengths, so in his view that would create a good balance. He cautioned that I needed to be clear about my goals in any relationship, and think about how to handle intimacy—not just sexual intimacy, he added, but emotional intimacy as well.

A few days after my first session with Mr. Haas, I returned to the dental facility for the installation of the flipper. I was amazed by the speed in which it had been made, but my spirits reacted immediately against this Barbie-doll device and the very visible metal bands holding it in. For now, though, I accepted it. "If this thing flew out during a singing performance, I'll look like Judy Garland in her hobo routine," I moaned to Gail. Another problem was that it covered my entire hard palate, leaving me lisping. Having to remind myself yet again of my luck to be alive and on a path to get healthier, I didn't complain—at least, not yet. But recent cancer survivors are a suspicious lot, always wary. I knew there had to be a more acceptable answer, a similar device that would not cross the forbidden midline of my head with metal, but something less cumbersome. It is a huge "no-no" in this form of holistic dentistry to cross the midline with metal, thought to have a possible effect on both co-ordination and brain function.

16

Hallelujah

I whistle a happy tune.
— Rodgers and Hammerstein, The King and I

As Dr. Rau got a better handle on me, he added items to my schedule as well as to my list of supplements. My appointment with Michael Falkner was one such addition. While I was sitting waiting for him at the dental building, a redheaded man with large, serious blue eyes appeared suddenly through a side door, sleeves rolled, blue button-down shirt tucked into khaki pants. He met me with such openness, exuding such a casual manner, that I was disarmed. But that first impression was misleading. Mr. Falkner is Mr. No-Nonsense, not a casual person at all.

He is an anthroposophic therapist, a long title that means he adheres to the teaching and principles of the late Rudolf Steiner. An Englishman by birth, he was raised in a small Kentucky town called Prospect. I worked with him twice during my second and third weeks at the clinic.

At that first appointment we retreated to his inner sanctum upstairs at the dental facility, chatting noncommittally. From the first, it was evident this man was somehow different from other "shrinks" I'd met. We discussed my history, though he probably knew most of it already. Then he asked me to make a list of what I really enjoyed doing, including things that gave me "joy and fulfillment." There were some moments of silence while I worked on it. My children and grandchild came first; then I wrote down hiking, music, nature, and reading as among my favorite activities.

Mr. Falkner glanced at the list and commented on some of the entries. "We have to be allowed to grow into the people we are supposed to be," my journal notes reveal. "To do that, we must often destroy or at least let go of some of what our parents gave to us." He meant their behavior, either genetically passed on, or mimicked after years and years of familiarity.

Sitting suddenly more upright, I felt cautious. There was an element of surprise here. Mr. Falkner's comment and facial expression reminded me of what Bobby Lewis said about the best actors, "You never know what they are going to do next." He wasn't acting, and he continued, speaking strongly and seriously. "We live in a spiritual context. Spiritual individuality has been growing in you, and now your process must include getting in touch with your essence, your individuality."

He continued to talk of spiritual growth and I began to cry. That was becoming an almost daily occurrence. For years, I had been so cut off from my emotions that I didn't cry easily, if at all. I was making up for that drought now, every day seeming to bring a catharsis of one kind or another. He said that an abused person feels, "I am just an object. It's not a question of what I think and feel; my emotions are not important.'" That all made sense to me. It was also heartening to hear him affirm that it was possible "to find yourself in an instant, when you are ready and the time is right." I was incredibly moved by his words and could hardly stop weeping.

When I said that I knew nothing about eurythmy, Mr. Falkner requested that I copy him in a simple exercise. Beginning to walk forward and then back, he instructed me to think of a flower opening to the sunshine and then closing at dusk. Walking forward, I was to close up, folding my arms across my chest. Stopping briefly, I was to return, walking backwards, arms open wide: reaching towards the sun, letting my chest expand, keeping my body position open, and letting my head stretch upward also.

During this sequence, he repeated a kind of mantra. I repeat it here in the exact words of the best Steiner translation. "Into my heart streams the power of the sun, into my soul works the warmth of the world. I will to breathe the power of the sun. I will to feel the warmth of the world. The warmth of the sun fills me; the warmth of the world permeates me." After I went forward and back three times, Mr. Falkner allowed that I wasn't great on the opening up part, but did closing down very well. That didn't surprise me.

It's difficult to describe the power of that small and simple exercise. Something in it reached me deeply; it was strangely relaxing, and has continued to be whenever I perform it.

Mr. Falkner had a way of asking really penetrating questions. He asked me to consider whether or not my illness had brought me more in touch with what had been wrong for me in my life, suggesting that it should free me up from negative attachments, allowing me to go forward with more time and energy for joy. These advances would in turn absolve me from my need to be in control. We both agreed that we are never in control anyway; we only think we are. I thought of the hair streaks lost to chemotherapy, my alter-ego Audi that had "insisted" I slow down. These were lessons in giving up control, not to mention the more dramatic lesson of the surgery. Not having succeeded entirely in leaving negative attachments behind was one of the reasons I was at the Paracelsus Clinic. But I was making progress.

With his usual candor, at the next session Mr. Falkner suggested that I ask myself what my goals were. I should focus on the future. "You should be relaxing, going slow, not fast, with quality, not quantity. Be aware of your space, be aware of time, but instinctively move into it, allowing yourself to go to a different space, and do it without a million distractions." The Audi must have emailed him, I thought ironically. He also linked nature and gardening, pointing out that the plant world "gets us in touch visually with the cosmic, digestible life cycle." If I could let go, I could stream right into that.

"You should embrace the sadness of what you've experienced because it will give substance, both to you now and then to whom and to what moves you," he said in conclusion. "It is important to become conscious of what your mission is and pay attention to the moment at which you make a connection." He helped me see that when the past came up, I had armored myself heavily by choice. But I didn't have to prove anything any more. Instead, I could relax more deeply, delve into the excitement of new things, keep discovering and learning, and live in the present. If I did these things, he knew I would emerge from the periphery into the center of my own life, no longer hiding or holding back.

Our work together was so helpful and profound that I asked him about following up. He gave me information on a center for anthroposophy in upstate New York, suggesting a teacher named Seth Morison. In lovely serendipity, on returning home I would find that Seth lived only forty minutes away from my house in Connecticut; I would work with him for several years.

Suddenly it was the day before I would leave—and the day of my last hyperthermia. For this one I brought my own music. The whale sounds wouldn't work for this occasion. *Gotterdammerung* was perhaps suitably dramatic, but I had Ella Fitzgerald and some orchestral music with me. Feeling like a veteran, I undressed, took the blue gown and lay down to wait for the IV, thermometer and heart monitor. The nurse this time was Claudia, a young strawberry blonde with a nice sense of humor and a quiet efficiency.

As the bed reached its full and incandescent temperature the heat became almost unbearable again. Claudia's watchful gaze reassured me throughout. As always, I had persistent questions. "Is my temperature rising? What is it, Claudia?" "Your temperature was very good this time. It's rising quickly, a sign of better regulation," she answered in good English. Closed off by the Velcro side attachments, with only the small rectangular peephole on top to let me see a tiny slice of the world, I found my claustrophobia inside this little "pod" returning.

Again, my father showed up, and again I began to cry. Yet, I had to let him know that all of his damage—his "shit," was the term I used—was his and his alone. "You need to take it. I have no use for it and don't want it," I told him. "I'm putting you behind me—in the past, but out where I can keep an eye on you." I thanked him for giving me my life, but sternly pointed out that he had tried to destroy me and take my innocence—and that none of it was my fault. It was very difficult, but I'm proud that I did it. Finally, he faded away, small and grieving. Glad and relieved, I felt my tears stop.

I was given some oxygen, helpful given how intense the experience had been. As I calmed down, positive and beautiful images appeared. I began to feel loving and joyful, imagining John building a garden with me. I was with my girls, loving them, observing the future. As Claudia turned off the heaters and the other paraphernalia was removed, I was in a different place and knew I'd always remember these treatments and their powerful effects.

That night, I packed up suitcases that were now full, even bulging. My mind and my heart were full as well. These had been three tough but fascinating weeks. It would take more time to let all the pieces of my personal jigsaw to fall into place, but I was leaving with a healthier body and mind, along with a solid beginner's understanding of the cells as the key to human health. One rogue cell had started the cancer, yes. But who I had been—emotionally, genetically, constitutionally, in terms of my life history—had started it.

I now saw myself a holistic being, multi-faceted, capable of improvement and integration. Surviving cancer and then choosing to experience these treatments had improved my self-esteem. I was proud of myself for coming to Paracelsus. I had taken a chance and been rewarded; the partnership between patient, doctor and therapist had worked well for me, as had the synergy of the clinic's varied approaches and treatments.

At Paracelsus I had screamed, sweated, cried, been infused with vitamins and minerals, cleaned up the "milieu," had colonics and reflexology, injected myself with mistletoe, taken a plethora of tests, lost teeth, and gained insight. I had experienced different heat treatments including the hyperthermias, during which I had dispatched my parents, more or less for good. I had discovered eurythmy and exorcised feelings of guilt I had never realized I had. My toxins had been drained, my cells were breathing better, and I had a great program of supplements and remedies to support my future wellness. Yale had done my physical surgery, but the emotional surgery had taken place here in Switzerland. It made sense; this was the place in which I felt safest. Karl Menninger's phrase "weller than well" came to my mind; I was beginning to understand viscerally what that meant.

Gail had gone back to Hawaii the week before. (She took with her an extra suitcase, full of ribbons that her sharp, prudent eye had spotted on sale in Lustmuhle.) As we said farewell, I knew we would meet again. Most of the people who had been there when I started the three weeks had left, but I managed goodbyes to my favorite nurses like Liselotte and Rita. Dr. Rau, Mr. Haas and Michael Falkner got special goodbyes and thanks. During our final meeting, Mr. Haas had given me an incredible good-bye present: a new meditation, "I'm a great Mom," which he described as a spiritual reality.

Packing finished, I paid my bill at the Schutzi, then said my goodbyes to Irene and a couple of other guests with a huge "farewell" reserved for the duvet. I would be taking the train to Austria for a short stay there. Swiss trains are one of the most amazing public transportation systems in the world, so efficient and clean you can hardly believe them. It would be a pleasure to give a dinner party in any of those railway cars, which are as obsessively clean as I like my kitchen to be. Now that I was a clinic veteran, next time I would take the train from Zurich rather than an expensive car service.

My suitcase was bursting with remedies and supplements, quinoa pasta, bottles of Dr. Hauscka's Lavender Bath Oil, pumpkin and sunflower seeds. I had my test results and a letter for customs asking that I be allowed to walk through some of the homeopathic medicines that might be affected by scanning machinery. The train conductor in St.

Gallen greeted me with a bit of a sour look when Christian, humming as always, handed over my mammoth beast of a suitcase. I gave Christian a hug and boarded the train, leaving a country that had done so much to improve my life. Again, however, I knew I'd be back, and that kept the nostalgia and tears at bay.

17

Salzburg

Life itself is the proper binge.

—Julia Child

As the train chugged gradually into Austria, the mountains standing as fortress-like companions along the way, I nestled peacefully into my plush seat. Out of the comfort zone of the Schutzi and the clinic, I'd have to go it alone. But I was looking forward to both my own and other people's reaction to this "new" person I was becoming. Were the changes real and permanent? I wasn't sure, but I was ready to find out. However, a few moments of nerves had hit me as I walked out of the Schutzi. As I reflected on the remarkable array of hotel guests I was leaving behind, all at different stages in their fights to regain their health, there was a bit of separation anxiety as well as my own concerns about leaving. I would miss the riotous dinners, the sharing of fear and the good conversation. I hoped luck would be in everyone's favor as I inwardly took my leave of them. The support from the daily mentoring was over, but I had my memory and my trusty little sketch book journal to help me remember their guidance.

I was going to Austria feeling more grounded, and even more sensual, than I had felt in a long time. The famous Salzburg Easter music festival lay in front of me. I was thrilled at the prospect, as this was something I'd wanted to do for a long time. "Don't postpone," one of

Bobby Lewis's aphorisms, had motivated me. This was my moment, one I was going to savor. I felt like a college kid on the loose at spring vacation, my energy exuberant. Across the aisle from me on the train were two teenage girls wearing clothes in Day-Glo colors, dangerously short skirts, and Goth nail polish. I felt surprisingly like them in some way, "high" on life and hope.

My American friend, Marion Bedrick, a veteran of the festival, had planned to join me in Salzburg. Instead, she had called me at the Schutzi to say that she had been involved in a taxi crash on her way to the airport and, though unhurt, would not be coming. But she'd already organized friends to be on the lookout for me, so I didn't feel alone.

The *Osterfest*, or Easter Music Festival, in the city of Mozart includes operas, concerts and lectures throughout the day and night. All over town, friends gather for lunch, tea, a drink or dinner in cafés and restaurants. Lively chatter about performances and favorite singers is audible everywhere, from one table to the next.

The elegant concierge at the Hotel Elephant also served as its receptionist and porter. While he cringed slightly at the size of my suitcase, he agreed to have my bed remade using sheets and blankets rather than a duvet. At last, maybe, I could get a good night's sleep. As the three of us—him, me and my monster valise—squeezed into the minuscule elevator, I wasn't sure which hat he was wearing.

The room was small but spotless. I now had both bathtub and toilet in the same room, as well as CNN for news. As I unpacked, I checked the drawers. Finding a Bible placed by the Gideons, I thought of Gail and her travails. My travel bag got quickly emptied, all the supplements lined up in military formation on the dresser and the mistletoe needles hidden under my lingerie in case room service thought I was a junkie.

Ah, Salzburg! A small city, it is formal in the European way. I went out for a walk before dinner. It was warm enough to be without a coat, though the sun was slowly slipping down behind the snow-capped peaks. I dined alone downstairs in the *rathskellar*, wistfully declining all of the bratwursts and knockwursts that were now forbidden to me, a small price to pay. I had no pain or stiffness of any kind throughout my body, and knew that my new diet choices and detox were a huge part of the cause. I felt physically as well if not better than I ever had; I had acquired tools and mantras to encourage me further, especially a greater awareness of being in the present moment. To spend five days listening to beautiful music was a joy. I didn't mind being alone; beauty and music would fill me.

Those three weeks in Switzerland had changed my life. The thinking behind this kind of medicine fascinated me. The principle idea that we are much more than the sum of our parts, a group of organs or systems, is so obvious, but is still not an intrinsic part of Western medicine's thinking. My emotional history was considered as important as my physical history, my build, my inner life, my general constitution and spirit, all parts were considered interconnected at root and dynamic levels.

But a big "however" was smugly facing me in a standoff. When a person has been conditioned by beliefs and experiences going way back, changing them suddenly or "seeing the light" creates internal empty space. Something has to fill it and replace what's being thrown out, in this instance, a lot of serious baggage. Even though the new ideas are better and healthier, it can take time to live them and make them ours. I wasn't aware of how all this would work, so part of me felt as if all the stale air had been replaced by high octane oxygen, very new and exciting but not yet focused.

After a good sleep in my crisp, starched sheets, I spent the next day—another one with nice shirt-sleeve temperatures—walking around. It was Good Friday and the church bells rang constantly. I ambled over to the famous Sacher Hotel to experience it, have tea and read the *International Herald-Tribune*, an essential when traveling. As I lowered myself onto the opulent red velvet booth, I dared to order a piece of the famed Sacher Torte—so much flagrant chocolate, chocolate and more dark chocolate that I was sure an alarm would go off and Dr. Rau's food police would appear. No one showed up, but I ordered a second pot of green tea to balance my sin of refined sugar, rationalizing that chocolate has lots of anti-oxidants, too. As I sat eating and reading the Pope's Easter message of peace and reconciliation, I knew that was what I also wanted, for me as well as the world.

I reveled at how much cleaner and clearer my mind was, the brain fog was gone, my concentration better than it had ever been. Since my inability to retain information had plagued me all through school, this clarity meant a great deal. I realized that anger and irritation at small things were distracting me less, no longer preventing me from enjoying inner calm. Now that I had "finished off" my parents in the hyperthermia, seeing both my father and my mother from a new and more empowering perspective, my guilt and anger seemed to have vanished. The empty space would fill up with better thoughts and happier memories.

I dressed carefully for the opera at the *Festspielehalle*, the opera house. Among other things I put a light film of mascara on my meager new lashes, now growing in again, and figured out how to pencil in slightly better eyebrows. It amused me that the first opera of the festival was *Turandot*, the first opera I had ever seen. How appropriate, for this second debut in the world; I was starting over, and giving old territory a re-tread was part of my plan.

The first time I had seen Puccini's opera about the icy Chinese princess, she had been sung by Maria Callas at the Metropolitan Opera in New York. This performance would be the best of the best, as the orchestra was the Berliner Philharmonic conducted by Claudio Abbado, who had recently fought off cancer of the stomach, a nasty diagnosis. There was a large crowd mingling in the opera house, but as I was alone, I hastened to my seat to wait for the first act curtain. My position afforded an excellent view. Watching Abbado conduct, I was struck by his energy, concentration and vigor. His connection to the musicians was so strong, I understood better what conducting is all about, the presence—the leadership and the connection. He and the musicians were totally in the present moment, sharing a Zen-like, rhythmic symbiosis.

Turandot is the story of a Chinese princess by the same name and Prince Calaf, a suitor who must answer three riddles. If he does, he wins the hand of the princess; if not, he faces execution. But Turandot is determined not to love any of her suitors, especially this handsome prince who has fallen in love with her on sight.

Addressing him coldly, she asks the first question: "What is born each night and dies each dawn?" Calaf answers correctly: "Hope." But hearing him, I thought, *No, no. You're wrong, Calaf. Without continued hope, we all die or give up. It's what keeps me and others going. Hope runs the world.* Uninhibited as I felt, I fortunately managed to keep it to myself. Naturally, Turandot melts and is transformed by love, and all ends happily. I wafted back to the Elephant, almost winking at the concierge. Up in my room I took my magnesium and zinc tablets and my herbal passionflower sleep drops. Sailing off to bed feeling warm, contented and positive, I was hoping to dream in Italian and very contented to have lovely sheets and blankets surrounding me.

The next morning in the dining room, ham and cheese slices beckoned from the breakfast table. Giving myself a gentle inner slap, I reminded myself of my detox duties: follow the program, alkalize the *milieu* and rejuvenate the cells. I trusted the clinic's warning that acidity is a cause of chronic illness and is exacerbated by ham, red meat, sugar, dairy products (except for occasional sheep's or goat's milk cheese), and almost anything, like chips, that is pre-made and packaged. The limitations felt hard that morning, but I followed them anyway.

That day, I met a few of Marion's friends, including a man who seemed interested, not only in opera, but in me. When he invited me to a big luncheon at his apartment across the river, quickly telling me the other guests' names, I was both amused and flattered. Did he think I expected to be the only guest? When I explained my dietary taboos, he suggested we go together to the outdoor market to load up on the right greens and veggies. Since that sounded like fun, off we started, back across the river.

This was a classic farmer's market with all sorts of produce available. The country women sported dirndl dresses, the farmers wore smocks and boots or clogs, the sun blazed. I already liked my new friend, Mel—he was bright and thoughtful. His luncheon party was fun, though I again firmly declined the salamis and cheeses begging for my attention. The other guests all being "operaphiles," I enjoyed listening to their knowledgeable talk. I agreed to go to the Parsifal with Mel. I felt flattered to have a nice guy interested and was attracted by his knowledge and love of opera and the twinkle in his eye. The attention so soon after the clinic underpinned my own feelings of wellness and the changes in me. It seemed my own energy had improved to the extent that I could be vibrant and even flirtatious.

Mel appeared to be a very bright, energetic man with a tremendous knowledge of, and passion for, the opera. That kind of intellect has always been a draw for me, and I was already wondering, "Could this be something for me?" I wasn't too clear about what he did, but his apartment was lovely and I appreciated the helpful spirit he had shown in wanting to go to the market with me. I felt I was back "in the game" of being attractive to men, without conditions; that is, I wasn't sick any more. John was always lurking in my head, but for right now, I thought, "Yes, who knows? This is fun and how life should be."

That night there were three short operas that I don't remember very well. I was alone. During an intermission, as I walked through the large lobby, I heard a voice I recognized say to a companion, "I don't believe it. This is truly a very old friend." I wheeled around and saw just that, a friend of many decades past, a passionate opera buff and a person of great charm. "Are you all by your little lonesome?" he smiled and asked. As it was so, he asked me to a dinner party for the next night, after the performance of Wagner's *Parsifal*. It would make for my latest night out in a long time, but it was an irresistible invitation. *Yes!* I thought. I would need that long dress my daughter Philippa and I had wrangled over during our packing marathon, and would have to tell Mel that I would have dinner plans after the performance.

For the previous ten months, subsumed by treatments and fighting fear, I had been, essentially, alone. I was now out safely on the other side on that solitary tunnel. In illness, you can't always plan; tomorrow can go either way. Now, once again, life was becoming more normal, more predictable. I knew what tomorrow, at least, would bring, and I was confident. I was living Dr. Rau's words about how dynamic and adaptable humans are. *I can self-repair and heal, react and adapt*, I thought. I had both the tools and the patience necessary.

Parsifal, Wagner's final completed opera, is taken from a medieval poem of the same name. Like a mystery play from that period, the six-hour opera is a story of suffering and redemption concerning the Holy Grail, allegedly Christ's cup from the Last Supper, and the Holy Spear, supposedly the first to pierce Jesus' side on the cross—two relics guarded by the Knights of the Grail. Somehow, this opera on this night seemed chosen with me in mind. I thought back with gratitude about the metaphysical and spiritual conversations with Mr. Falkner, which had awakened my spirituality again.

Parsifal is considered a "young fool", an innocent. The first thing the audience sees is a swan, dropping with a crash onto the stage. It has been shot and killed by Parsifal, who is unaware that swans are sacred to the Knights. John and I had had a lovely pair of trumpeter swans living on our pond in Connecticut. To my mind, black-beaked trumpeters are among the most beautiful of all swans. They were wonderful to watch approaching each other, necks flexing, synchronizing to be in the same position as they make the shape of a heart. They are vegetarian, lack teeth and mate for life, the first two qualities resonating. I hadn't mated for life, but I had begun to forgive myself, and to better understand why that hadn't happened. The dead swan of the opera briefly upset me, as I didn't want it to be a metaphor for any future possibilities.

That night, sitting with Mel, I was again utterly riveted: by Claudio Abbado, the costumes and sets, the story, and one of singers. The role of Amfortas, guardian of the sacred relics, was sung by Thomas Quastoff. A very short man with almost no arms, he was clearly a victim of thalidomide, but he possessed a voice that could only have been created by the gods. I could hardly imagine the obstacles this man had needed to overcome; the physical and psychological frustrations had to have been enormous. Between Abbado, Quastoff, the swan and the story, I felt overwhelmed. Humbled by what Quastoff and Abbado had been able to do, I could almost feel discipline and direction pointing their sinuous fingers at me.

I happened to be seated next to Quastoff at dinner one night during my stay. He was open, approachable and strong. But he utterly astonished me when he pulled out a pack of Marlboros and offered me a smoke. When I asked him how an opera singer dared do that, he said something like, "You gotta do what you gotta do," in his booming, bass-baritone voice. I had no response, as I was totally stunned, and politely refused. He was a charming dinner companion. His face was so interesting; there was great intelligence in the eyes and in the length of the brow. I also saw pain and something else, maybe longing, maybe anger. The way his Thalidomide-damaged hands worked was fascinating. Their skill appeared to be effortless as he drew out and lighted the cigarette. What a man. He was a titan in what he'd done with his life.

The festival wound down and people began to leave the city. As I repacked my giant bag, I counted my big adventure back into the world as a success. I'd felt well and energetic, had fun with both old and newer friends, stayed happy, and followed my diet despite temptation. Mel and I were on the same plane to London and we agreed to keep in touch, which we did for a while.

I flew back to New York via London so I could see Anastasia and Stefan and help with their wedding plans. She and I checked out florists, cake makers, and the church, read catering menus, looked at accommodations for family and friends, and talked about dresses. She had researched everything wonderfully, so it was really all done except for a few choices. It was a special time—even more so because I had become deeply fond of Stefan, and knew she'd made a great choice in her husband-to-be.

18

Life, the Universe and Everything Else

Life is washed in the speechless real.

—JACQUES BARZUN

Back in New York, it seemed that everyone I ran into was amazed at how well and healthy I looked. I liked hearing that, but it didn't surprise me—well and healthy was how I felt.

Because I had changed, my life in Manhattan had changed. I decided to sell my apartment there and move full-time to the country. The reason was not only to try to understand what the last year had been for me, but to have real down time for introspection, more than the summer had provided. My active social life in the city now seemed empty and featureless. Years before, one of the therapists I had seen suggested that I needed to spend more time alone. But to me back then, time alone was not having a dinner date. Now I was more ready to create that opportunity.

Spring was lovely in Connecticut. Remembering Mr. Falkner's suggestions about connecting to the plant cycle and the seasons, I offered my services at a small greenhouse-nursery near my house. There I got "down and dirty" with the soil. Among other things, I learned to repot seedlings, to be gentle and careful not to break new shoots or interrupt their growth into strong plants. The connection seemed obvious: I was repotting myself, too, and wanted to support my "new shoots."

April turned into May. I stuck with my diet, drank lots of water, and took my supplements religiously. I got used to saying "no, thank you" to desserts or pork and other delicious, acid-bearing foods when out to dinner. I could more or less manage the rest of the instructions, including rules such as Dr. Rau's dictum not to eat any fruit after four in the afternoon because of fermentation in the gut, which causes acidity and overworks the liver. The health store in Woodbury, Connecticut, saw a lot of me. Bags of veggies piled on my counters, I'd wash, spray and grate carrots, daikon radish and tons of zucchini to make the raw salads I had enjoyed for lunch at Winkelstein's back in my clinic days. For dinner, I'd often make Dr. Rau's alkaline soup. It combined green beans, zucchini and celery, cut up and boiled in water till soft, then liquidized; a potato is allowed in winter, and a shake of Himalayan salt. It was surprisingly delicious, especially with a drop or two of olive oil. Eating so much produce daily, along with healthy additions such as flax oil, I felt like a veggie rock star.

But one piece of the healing was not going well at all. The dental "flipper" that was supposed to solve all problems of my missing front tooth was a constant frustration. It not only wiggled noticeably but completely covered the roof of my mouth, depriving me of the taste and texture of food and drink. My patience dwindling, I kept breaking the device, spending too much to get it fixed or replaced. If this was supposed to balance me, it was doing the reverse.

I thought about those disappeared root canals and the epiphany I'd felt when the front tooth went. I didn't doubt Dr. Rau's belief that root-canalled teeth were dead teeth "like stones, but mainly pulp or organic mass which connect to the lymph system," gathering bacteria that couldn't easily be flushed out. So I knew that the decision to have them removed was the right one. There just had to be something better than the flipper. I put the word out to Gail on Kauai, hoping that this resourceful goddess could suggest a solution.

John and I were seeing each other for dinner sometimes, though we were certainly not back together. He could, however, recognize a vibrant, more relaxed ex-wife, a woman more like the person he thought he had originally chosen to marry. Seeing my changes, he became very interested in my tales of the clinic. Dr. Rau would be back at the Marion Institute in May, and we decided that we'd drive up together for the seminar. John would be facing a knee replacement in September. He thought maybe the clinic might have a different approach, something helpful to add to the conversation.

So off we went, staying at a nice bed and breakfast in Marion, all chintz and potpourri. We were virtually the only civilians amid a crowd of health practitioners, from Maine all the way to California, who had heard about the unique approach called Biological Medicine. Dr. Rau and his fellow speakers were really fascinating that weekend, often keeping me on the edge of my seat.

One of the lectures focused on Dr. Rau's concept of "life themes." It was an unusual talk, with unusual concepts, based on the core tenet of Traditional Chinese Medicine: that everything connects and all systems, cells and tissues have a relationship to each other. I still don't pretend to understand the life theme material perfectly, but it fascinates me and has its own clear logic.

As most people know, Chinese medicine is based on five elements—wood, fire, earth, metal and water—and that they relate to each other in mutually beneficial and circular patterns. Wood promotes fire, fire earth, earth promotes metal, metal water, and water helps to generate wood and to extinguish fires. To the Chinese, these elements also relate to the concepts of dynamism and constant change. According to Dr. Rau, there are five seasons: spring, early summer, late summer, autumn and winter. Not only plants but humans have a life cycle which can be viewed through the seasons. We flow up and down, sprouting, growing, fading and dying and we repeat this cycle in different ways every year.

As it pertains to the individual, Dr. Rau explained that each season has its own character and meaning. Spring was strong, not stable, more self-oriented. Summer brought stability to one's life and growth. "Late summer is the fruit carrier and in the autumn, the leaves fall down." And winter, the end of the cycle, is when things die down so that new life can begin again. Developing harmonically, a balanced individual passes through all of these seasons as would a plant, he explained, growth and expansion being the determining factors.

He described his medicine as an approach that looks at inner as well as outer growth. He emphasized that though he uses the meridians and their connection to organ systems to diagnose, it is never the organ alone which becomes ill, but always the whole human being. He made it very clear that he and his colleagues look for the multi-causality of disease, "an individualized combination of causes in any one patient." He described looking at patients, when diagnosing, as being weak in the direction of a particular disease, and commented as well that he believed there is almost always an emotional component in the development of cancer. I found the last part of his explanation very moving when he said that our fulfillment in life includes our gathered wisdom which bears fruit, "which is the purpose of nature, after all. But the power of true healing is in our hearts."

People who get sick are people who have become arrested in one of the seasons. Not having developed that season's dynamic expectations in the right time line, one of the annual cycles from spring to winter, they get stuck in a "constitutional" weakness. That made perfect sense to me, and I listened avidly as he explained it more deeply.

Someone who does not find the stability, love and partnership associated with their season will get sick, Dr. Rau commented, and the illness will relate to the organ of the season. In Switzerland, he had said I was a 'winter,' and my illness, ovarian cancer, was related to winter as well—winter issues including not only bladder and kidney illness, but also diseases of the ovaries and uterus. As Dr. Rau was speaking, I was scouring the printout sheets to see what else it said about kidney/bladder meridian types. The expectation of winter, "a beautiful season" as the handouts said, is that "the individual will go back to warm, cozy behavior; it is a time to return to family and the security inherent in family life. In winter it is necessary that we conserve the fruit and seed until the spring; the seed will propagate the family."

If the winter meridian is in balance, the person is "energetic, clever, powerful and ambitious…with an inner drive from deep within, with strong willpower…also philosophical, curious and likes to play with ideas." But when out of balance, winter may bring "difficulty with relationships and commitment, a person who remembers slights forever, is argumentative, lacks ambition, is 'stuck' because of fear, terror or panic" and feels resignation, due to fear of life."

Oh dear, I thought, that seemed to describe the 'old' me pretty well. On the other hand, the devilish inner voice chimed, "Sweetie, *no* one in your family has been good about commitment." The good news was that I could now recognize both the condition of being in balance and the moments when I was not.

John and I were both impressed by the seminar. After the weekend, we decided we'd go to Switzerland for two weeks in June to be treated; after that, we'd visit London briefly and then go up to Scotland. For several years, he had rented a 19th-century place there, an old pile of stone, stucco and fireplaces that we both loved.

Back at home, I spent a lot of time revisiting Steven Forrest's reading of me. His description of "getting stuck" jibed with Dr. Rau's concept. All summer, I reflected and transcribed the tapes. Each time I reread the pages I learned something new, constantly struck by the similarities between his ideas and those of the clinic. This was a moment when everyone was saying the same thing. I had to listen—I'd be a fool if I didn't.

Like the doctor, Steven had emphasized the risks of getting stuck, though he spoke not in terms of seasons but of the shells associated with Cancerians. A Cancer's shell needed to be discarded at the right time in order to move forward rather than stall. To be true to myself, he said, I needed time alone by myself with no distractions. "You need to put up a shell between yourself and the world," the reading explained.

Steven saw me as having three roads from which to choose. I could be "a magnet for chaos or learning" or could attempt a "quest for stability or safety." But more preferable in his eyes would be to "understand the ever-expanding complexity of the universe." That would be the most difficult path. I had already experienced chaos, too much of it for too long. I wanted all three, but stability and safety were paramount for now. Once I had established myself, he added, "You will go into the world and get curious. When you are old, conservatives will be afraid of you." That made me chuckle as I thought, "what is probably truer is that I am not afraid of them!" The 11th house, he continued, "is the house for late bloomers, and you have a tremendous 11th house. The work you've come to do is not the work of a younger woman." The statement seemed to buy me time, mitigating feelings of youth lost and time passed. To be an elder whose work lay ahead gained me a new lease on life. The empty spaces were beginning to fill!

"Love is dangerous for you, as you are the epitome of sensitivity. You enter into relationships that you think are safe, but the only relationship that has a prayer of lasting for you is one with a spiritual basis. You need, but also fear intimacy, and can be hurt very badly." These were broadside hits, but I knew they were true as I looked at my past.

Amid all these reflections, life went on. Yale asks patients to come every three months in the first year after their surgery for blood work and a physical, internal exam. That spring, the conclusion was so far, so good. The blood test results were acceptable. Although my CEA, a cancer diagnostic, came in a little high, neither Dr. Schwartz nor Karen, the chemo nurse, were worried as long as it didn't spike up suddenly. The chemo-induced neuropathy in the tips of my fingers and toes had disappeared, something Dr. Schwartz had hoped would happen, but rightly hadn't guaranteed.

I also drove down to see a practitioner of biological medicine in Pennsylvania a couple of times. An earlier test had revealed I was losing calcium from my bones, a potential side effect from chemo, stress, the loss of estrogen, and my physical type, which is naturally osteoporosis prone. Dr. Zieve suggested doing hair tests which confirmed the bone loss. We worked on that for a time, adding more supplements. Though I found him an excellent physician, the drive was too lengthy and I was getting overwhelmed working so hard at getting well. I had plenty of guidance and tools. Maybe, I thought, I should just stay still and relax more.

I was finding that the farther away in time I traveled from the disease, the less obsessed I was about it. Dr. Rau's diet and supplements had removed cravings for wrong foods like sugar; the theory being that if I craved sugar, I was missing essential nutrients in my diet. I was sweating more easily and had more energy, although I still had to pace myself; I was calmer and stronger physically. My sympathetic nervous system was winding down from the constant "fight or flight" mechanism, though I still had to watch getting hyper about small things.

Before leaving for that second visit to Switzerland, I felt it was time to check in with John Postley. Much as I loved him, I had been avoiding him. I sat reading the newspaper before my 8:30 a.m. appointment when all of a sudden, I felt someone looking at me. "Get into my office and sit down," he said, the ubiquitous humor in his eyes. Following him into his office, always filled with photos, patient folders and artwork, I sat down in my usual chair.

"When you told me you were going to Switzerland to a clinic, I thought you were crazy," he said. "I saw no reason for it; you had beaten cancer. Now that I see you, I know you did the right thing. Tell me about it."

That meant a great deal to me. He was such a wonderful doctor. I trusted him deeply, although we didn't always agree. He told me not to worry about the CEA; it would have to be in the stratosphere for him to be concerned. I cringed just a bit as I told him I was going back to the clinic. But he said little about it, except that he thought I had beaten the disease and was well. Again, we agreed to disagree. As we said goodbye, I said I'd check in with him on my return.

During those months, the inner support and belief from Mr. Haas's mantra for me, "I can give and receive love," grew. He had understood the loneliness and sadness I had felt throughout many parts of my life and how the loving instinct in me had been blunted by my family experiences, my first marriage, and my loss of the ability to trust. It surprised me how strengthening such a simple sentence could be; the key, I realized, was that it had come from someone I could respect.

To love well, to trust, and to try to forgive were now my priorities, things I continue to work at today. Back then I would sometimes find myself in tears as I reread my diary and Steven Forrest's notes. To my amazement, I realized it was because I was happier, relieved of inner burdens, feeling the changes both physically and emotionally. I thought back to Dr. Candace Pert, who I've mentioned earlier in this book, and her descriptions of the science behind the idea that emotion is stored in the body's cells as well as the brain. My release of stored and repressed grief and anger had cleaned up my cells as well as my soul. I felt it, and began enjoying the wonder of simple relaxation afforded by living more in the moment, rather than being constantly distracted by tomorrow or yesterday.

The other Mr. Haas mantra was, "You are a great mom." This may or may not have been true, but it was also in sync with my healing process, as it touched on a higher dimension than day-to-day living, with the distractions and conflicts that may affect behavior. That wise interjection let me access my better spirit of motherhood and the desires I had for my children while I was raising them, especially during the very difficult years as a single mother in London.

19

The Past is a Foreign Country

Even a god cannot change the past.
— ATTRIBUTED TO AGATHON,
ATHENIAN TRAGEDIAN

My second visit to the clinic was similar to the first, with the customary infusions, a re-evaluation of the supplements, and appointments with Dr. Rau, Mr. Falkner, and Mr. Haas. John proved a real trooper. He went along with all the clinic's recommendations with such gusto that I was impressed and happy about his trust and intuition.

My birthday fell during that visit. John found out about a special hotel and took me to the Posthaus for the weekend to celebrate. The Posthaus is a short drive from Lustmuhle in Lec, Austria. A historic chalet painted both inside and out with beautiful murals, it had the most elegant breakfast of anywhere I've ever eaten. It would have been Dr. Rau's delight, as the offerings were replete with nuts, seeds, freshly baked spelt bread, homemade jams, muesli and yogurt from the hotel's own kitchens. The table settings were presented artfully as well, with lovely silver jam pots, starched napkins and tablecloths, and local flowers in small pots among the *naperie*.

Even though Europe was having a heat wave, I walked for miles on the grassy, hilly trails, talking to the brown cows and shouting "the hills are alive..." to each "Bessie." I made a grand loop, knee deep in wildflowers, listening to the cowbells enlivening the soft Alpine breezes. As I checked in with my own energy, I felt that it was boundless, not nervous, and that my emotional temperature was good, too.

Though we had a nice time, John was unapproachable emotionally, a mystic tomb of silence. *Where do you want to have dinner? I need to fill up the car. This muesli is delicious:* those were our exchanges. His head was usually in a book, because he is not a walker or hiker. Besides, I wasn't seeking resolution or more than companionship just then, and I was probably a bit guarded. His distance left me kind of curious and suspended. Over that weekend, I felt, at times, angry with him for not communicating more. In hindsight, I think we were both trying to take a closer look at the relationship without taking a closer look. Still, we both felt and seemed well as we headed for Scotland. There, the heat is never too *much*. Scotland will never be the New Tuscany!

It turned out that the weather in Scotland was beautiful, warm and with clear, big skies. John fished for salmon and I walked. We saw friends and people seemed relieved to see that we were together and that I was well; John was visibly pleased by both reactions. We were circling each other a bit in familiar surroundings. It had its humorous side, as I was no longer the lady of the house, but I was still Mrs. Horn.

After Scotland, a happy, mostly easy time for both of us in a place of comfort, helping with Anastasia's wedding was my number one concern. I was charged only with getting the bridesmaids' dresses as well as visiting Philippa and finding something for her and Miranda to wear. In a way, that was difficult. My former husband was running the show, and show it was to be. The wedding would be in a cathedral, the reception at the Victoria & Albert Museum, with a seated dinner and dancing. That was fine and wonderful, but I had no real part in it. My relationship with him was really non-existent, much as I had tried to create some kind of conversation.

However, Anastasia has an enormous talent for diplomacy. In her way, she made me feel important to the process. That meant a lot.

This was the last wedding for my daughters. I was craving some sense of getting along and having fun with it, fraught as I know all weddings can be.

During one final pre-wedding trip to London, Anastasia and I found a restaurant where John and I could host a lunch after the wedding, planned not only for the out of town guests, but also for the bride and groom. They wanted to visit with their friends, many who'd come from very far away places, including Hong Kong. Afterward, they'd leave on their wedding trip.

The wedding of the last child is a big deal for a mother—at least, I thought so. She's "officially" out of a job then, even if the kids are all grown up. No more family vacations or school holidays to make it all come right. I would have time back in Connecticut to work all these feelings out. Anastasia and I went over the flowers and visited cake makers. She had it all well under control, both watching the bottom line and designing the look she wanted. She pictured the bridesmaids in velvet capes with their own clothes underneath. I thought the capes could easily be done in the States, especially as I'd have more time to work on them. Meanwhile, I was discovering the role of elder to be a good place to search for the rest of my life. I saw the truth as a snapshot. Time passes quickly—more quickly, it seems, the older you get. Sixty becomes seventy in a minute.

I came back to the Bethlehem house short on ideas of what to wear as the mother of the bride at an evening wedding in London. My feelings were tied up with the aftereffects of my illness, including its impact on my hair. I also wanted to convey some sort of elder, matriarchal strength, if only for show. If I wasn't truly there yet, I was trying my best.

The right look would be Russian, I thought, as the wedding would be in the Russian Cathedral. I loved those Dr. Zhivago clothes, none of which I thought I had until I rifled my closet one afternoon. The perfect dress emerged from the dusty interior, a long rosy-pink frock with long sleeves. It had dignity, was pretty, and was dead simple, just the ticket. I prowled around and found a pretty coat with a little fur band, which ended up as the perfect combination. I was ready, age-appropriate and color-coordinated.

The Russian Orthodox ceremony included crowns for both bride and groom, held over their heads for long periods by chosen grooms-men. As Stefan is 6'8", selection for his team went to the potential basketball players in the group. The service is long, with chanting and incense. There is no seating. The mother of the bride enters on her own, walking to a designated pace. Tears were welling up even before I arrived. I couldn't contain myself, though it was just tears, no sobbing. So much raced through my head; I felt both the losses of my past and a sense of relief. A month or two of delay in my cancer diagnosis and I might not have made this wedding. I shed tears of joy just being there.

Seeing my daughter marry touched my heartstrings with relief. I thought Stefan was so right for her—they were right for each other. I liked his family, seeing strength, cohesion and love in their interactions.

John looked very elegant in his morning coat, as did my brother Llewellyn. They were my support system, along with Miles, Llewellyn's partner. John had been a wonderful stepfather, supportive and generous to the girls, never overstepping into the father role. Looking like an El Greco figure, Father Alexander gave a homily full of praise for this special couple, wishing for the blessings of children and happiness as they stood quietly, holding candles and with their crowns above their heads.

The reception was seamless with dinner, many toasts, lots of champagne, and dancing, too. Anastasia had persuaded a tenor friend to deliver Italian love arias before dinner. John and I walked back to our hotel exhausted. Before parting to go to our rooms, we agreed that it had gone very well, a celebratory hug marking our goodnight. The next day, a large group of us met up and dug into the curries, dal and pappadoms as if we hadn't eaten in days. We all swapped stories from the night before, including how hard it was to hold the obligatory crown over Stefan's head during the long ceremony.

Then it was back home to rest and make plans for Christmas. I had set myself up, inadvertently, for a fall, and found myself feeling rather abandoned. After all of the seemingly familial festivities in London, I guess I assumed there were more to follow. Phillipa and "her" John had other plans, however, and Anastasia and Stefan were in London, of course. I really didn't expect too much from "my" John, though I thought we might build on the time we'd spent together over the last months. It came as a surprise to have him say, "Don't count on me for Christmas." It turns out he was still trying to figure out an existing relationship. Christmas had always been my favorite holiday, but this year I was tired, more emotionally than physically. Also, I was lonely, in need of comfort and company.

My stalwart friend Lou Miano came through for the day itself, inviting me to have Christmas lunch with his brother Richard and his wife, Lynn, who lived near me and who had been wonderful to me during the summer of chemotherapy. Richard is a fabulous cook and we gorged on a great Italian Christmas feast with endless trimmings and courses, Dr. Rau's diet forgotten for a day. Mrs. Miano, Lou's mother, was there, vibrant and totally on the ball in her nineties. The day with them made up for a lot.

A snowstorm raged outside. Despite it, after lunch I said my thank-yous and climbed into the faithful Audi. I had decided to drive up to Cambridge, Massachusetts to spend a few days with Karin Stephan, a friend and yoga guru who runs a loft apartment-*cum*-bed and breakfast. As the benevolent dictator of this small commune, Karin welcomes people with a desire for quiet and contemplation—an interest in yoga not required. She seems to attract people going through a period of vulnerability in their lives. That difficult Christmas, she gave me the sanctuary I needed to work out my emotional "stuff."

With the snow pelting down the drive was horrendously crazy, demanding both concentration and guts. Even with slippery roads I had to drive on the offense, as there were many trucks on the road, changing lanes and spewing snow up onto the windshield in big, wet clumps. I questioned my sanity somewhat during that drive; the alter ego Audi provided no answers, presumably too busy with the roads to help.

Karin Stephan is a pocket Venus, petite and blonde. She is an inspiring, excellent teacher and a most loving, sensitive and intuitive woman. I respect her more than any yoga teacher I have ever worked with. A onetime student of B.K.S. Iyengar himself, she strictly follows his school of yoga, using its characteristic props to work on alignment and structure. She possesses an extra dimension when it comes to understanding people's bodies; she can tell where tension is held and release it with a tiny adjustment. Beyond her role as healer, we share a long friendship—she is a good listener who knows both my girls and John, too.

I was trying to understand the reasons I felt so gutted. I think that having experienced the traumatic loss and death of a parent early in life, before I was really able to understand and deal with it, had made me highly reactive in times of vulnerability. Also, I regretted not having the chance to go over the wedding with John, laughing and talking about all the things we'd seen and shared. But I am a person who can be alone, and always figure out a way to fill in the blanks. Being with Karin was a wonderful choice, as she understands everything. She was happy to hear about the wedding, as she loves Anastasia, and was sympathetic to my feelings of loneliness and abandonment at this time.

The main room of Karin's place is a huge, colorful loft. It serves as teaching area, kitchen, library and performance space, with the Stephwan family Steinway lodged with dignity in a corner. Karin hosts evenings of music or poetry; I did my very first cabaret show in that space, all dressed up in long green velvet, scared to death, my center of gravity somewhere in the stratosphere. That had been a pivotal evening. At the end of the forty minute show, I had realized that I hadn't died and that one woman in the audience had a tear in her eye after my rendition of *La Vie en Rose*, so performing never scared me much again. (I realize her tears could have been from hearing the French language massacred, but I choose to think otherwise.)

The room across the hall from my bedroom belonged to Nancy, Karin's full-time tenant, a masseuse specializing in Indian hot stone treatments. Since it was Christmas, she wasn't fully booked. Twice I stepped across the hall and climbed eagerly onto her massage table. The room was chilly but she swiftly and professionally covered me with soft towels before beginning the massage with my back. The stones, black and of various elongated shapes, had been heated in hot water. Nancy took one in each hand and slid them deftly across my skin, producing a scent redolent of Christmas—cinnamon, nutmeg, and no doubt frankincense and myrrh. I just adored massage; I always had, since my very first experience of it when my mother let me have my first massage at Elizabeth Arden's New York salon when I was twelve or thirteen.

Nancy mentioned that she too was a recent survivor of cancer. That surprised me, because she couldn't have been more than thirty. She described herself as in remission, a bit of cancer lingo that always gets my attention. Far be it from me to judge anyone's syntax or usage; each of us has to decide how to deal with both illness and its aftermath in the way that is best for us. But in my cancer, there is no room for ambiguity. I prefer specificity. "Remission," defined as "a decrease or subsidence (especially a temporary one)," is equivocal, and that's enough for me to drop the word. In contrast, Nancy felt that it alerted her to remain hyper-vigilant about her illness.

After that exchange, we talked no more. My approach coming into the room had been rather warlike. I wanted to exhaust any cancer cells, let them know I was a fighter just in case they got any ideas. But as the mysterious, elemental stones and Nancy's rhythmic motion washed the oil over me, the scent transported me into a quieter, dreamier place, my own little asteroid of calmness and silence.

Another resident was Alees, a Dutch woman from Amsterdam who had been the chef at Karin's most recent Florida workshop. This macrobiotic chef *extraordinaire* produced a stream of the most sublime and varied food from what seemed like the world's smallest kitchen.

It was hard to believe that something so delicious was good for you, too.

This was a unique time, with only myself to think about, in a sanctuary of sorts with calm in every aspect of every part of the day. My nervous system had needed this; I had been in overdrive. Karin, massage, yoga, macrobiotic food, and solitude by choice had gotten me to a state of calm both physically and psychically. I wasn't as upset as when I arrived. This was the winter season, the season of warmth, a time of coming together back to the family and a time of rest, death and rebirth. My girls were grown women with lives of their own, their futures in front of them. Karin helped me see that I was still emotionally frail and needed strengthening. My constant thinking about things I couldn't change or return to wasn't helping me. I needed to do more of what I'd heard in Switzerland: to go and figure out how to nurture myself and stay in present, real time.

Those four days over Christmas became another turning point. I went into them struggling, still holding on to the past for dear life. By the time I left, I had reached a quieter place of peace and acceptance. My heart needed more healing, and I was still a work in progress, but I could acknowledge the place I was in, and that it was a better place than I'd ever been before. I had always understood that life doesn't always work out how you think it should or how you want it to. Maybe you are wrong, anyway, and haven't figured it out properly. Maybe life has a better plan. Whatever it was, I would deal with it. Besides, I had always felt, in some positive way, guided.

As I left Karin's, I had much on which to reflect. From March to December, I had turned myself around quite a bit. The "new" me was real. The relationship with John was still a conundrum, but in time, it would resolve itself and I would understand it better and where it was going. The empty spaces inside me were not yet healed, but I was making progress. Most importantly, perhaps, I was now embracing myself and my existence as an "elder." I was a woman who would no longer deny, ignore, or stay silent about her feelings and beliefs.

20

Right Turns

Unless we change direction, we are likely to end up
where we are headed.

— OLD CHINESE PROVERB

As 2003 dawned, two 'big' ideas emerged. The first was to get out
of the house in Bethlehem and cut my losses on it, both emotional and
financial. Bethlehem, lovely as it was, just wasn't right for me.

If I did manage to sell the house, I was toying with the idea of a
move to New Haven, a great university town with lots of interesting
people and activities and a place where I had friends. There I might
both finish my Bachelor of Arts degree, an enduring long-term wish,
and maybe create a new life. From New Haven, I could easily travel
in to New York to see friends or soak up some culture—the train
connections were good. I wouldn't be that far from John's farm in
Washington Depot or from Bridgewater, where "my" room at the
Kinsolvings' house was always ready. The proximity to Yale, i.e. Dr.
Schwartz, probably played its part in this design for living. Though I
wouldn't end up pursuing this plan, back then the idea was something
to hold on to as I was rethinking my life.

My second decision was to act on something which had been brew-
ing in my mind since the end of chemo. I'd been lucky—had been
spared. That held almost mystical meaning for me. I wanted to write

a book about going through the process, telling why I believed I'd done well. Its main mission would be to help women become more proactive in facing the challenges of a difficult diagnosis, a possible recurrence, and even just aging itself. If I could help reassure women that they had choices regarding their care and well-being, share my insights on illness and healing, and describe my experience with the complexity and length of recovery, I would feel I'd made a positive contribution. Though the project would take many more years to come to fruition, it was an energizing, inspiring idea even then.

In the meantime, the winter was rough, with endless, heavy snow-falls. I felt lonely and isolated. I was working on filling those new, empty spaces in my psyche that had been revealed in Switzerland. But other than Gail and Susan, there was no one close to me who truly understood this process and/or was willing to spend time talking. Besides, I wanted to be with someone who'd "been there", like Gail. I was reluctant to burden friends who were engaged in just living their daily lives, not focusing on thoughts of illness and survival.

I decided that visiting Gail on Kauai would be the perfect way to escape the cold exterior world and the emotional chill of the house. I also wanted to see how she was doing and give support where needed. She'd offered an open-ended invitation. Waiting out the eight hour time difference so that I could phone at a civilized nine a.m. Hawaii time, I dialed. Gail answered right away. She said she would be happy to receive me at any time. "Just come," she added.

I booked a flight for March. I planned to break the trip in LA for a couple of days staying with a friend, then go to Pebble Beach on the Monterey Peninsula to pay a brief visit to a former boyfriend—the person in my life just before I met John. I felt a need to reach out, to revisit people in my past. I was especially focused on those with whom there had been glitches, who weren't quite right at the time or who had been close but with whom I'd lost touch. I was trying to better understand my past and to create a time line of big events or turnings in my life where something or someone had caused me to change.

The Pebble Beach visit was an eye opener for me. When I left at the end of two days, I couldn't believe I had spent two years seeing that man. He was still undeniably handsome and charming, and had been so glamorous in his past New York life. Now, meeting him in the midst of so much deep work on my identity, he seemed rather sad and empty to me. I had really changed.

Sipping a glass of Merlot on the Continental flight from Los Angeles to Kauai, I reflected back on that time in my past, wondering whether there had been much substance to that relationship. But mostly I was focused on the future, and pondering the kind of book I wanted to write. It felt slightly daunting. But I knew my story, and I was now armed with a fierce commitment to sharing what I knew of recovery, prevention of recurrence, and vitality and dynamism in aging. However, I'd never written much other than college papers and some advertorials for *Town and Country* magazine. Still, with my laptop, a brand new will, and a fresh focus, I was ready to go. Gail would be completely supportive, I knew.

Before falling asleep briefly on that five hour flight, the plane's engines humming, I imagined the visit. Gail and I would just spend time together, and talk about everything--except religious beliefs. Gail was an Evangelical Christian and I, an Episcopalian of the old school. Curious about Raymie, her husband, and her adored son, Raymond, I looked forward to meeting both. Relaxing in a beautiful place, focusing my energy, and beginning to write in a house where only friendship was expected: it was just what I needed right then.

A dusk landing in Honolulu proved smooth. Stepping down off the aircraft, I was hit by a burst of frangipani or something equally fragrant. I walked over to the in-transit waiting room for the "puddle jumper" to Lihue, Kauai's small airport. At Kauai, the northernmost of the Hawaiian Islands, we were greeted with leis and an endless line at the Avis rental office. When my turn arrived, impulsively, I asked for a Jeep. Somehow, a Jeep signified youth and playfulness. John always talked about the fun he'd had growing up on Nantucket with his Wrangler. Why shouldn't I try it too? So I left the airport in a white Wrangler with an unaccustomed gear shift.

A quick call to the Miller household fortified me with additional directions to the house. I headed off to Waimea, where Gail lived. The uninhabited, unlit road seemed to be passing through vast sugarcane plantations—at least, they were sugar cane if my nose was right. When Hawaiians give instructions, I was learning, they say things like, "Go past the third palm tree after the green house on the right and make a left." It's all completely clear to them, though anxiety-producing for those of us used to more populated areas and GPS devices.

Nevertheless, it seemed to work. After about forty five minutes, I made a right turn into well-lit grounds. Out rushed Gail, Raymie and a big dog. As I jumped out of the Jeep, Gail placed another lei over my tired head, this one thick and rich with fragrant blooms that she had specially ordered just for me. We hugged, both deeply happy to see the other. In the house dinner was waiting—a sumptuous feast, resplendent. The generosity and style were so typical of Gail. Eating on their front porch, I reveled in the nearness of the Pacific, a short walk from the house. The waves rhythmically crashed against the rocks only yards away, sublime and hypnotic. The silken air flooded my senses with the joy of reunion and the surprise of Hawaii, despite my travel fatigue.

Gail looked much the same as she had in Switzerland. She was not a tall woman, about five foot three, with a petite and lovely figure and very pretty face. Her eyes were striking and expressive, large amber orbs framed by a fringe of dark, thick lashes, eyes incapable of guile. She looked healthy and tanned, so I couldn't read anything from her appearance. Raymie, her husband, was handsome, also tanned, blue-eyed, and mustached. I would learn that he was dedicated to the perfect wave, and usually off in the early hours surfing with his cohorts.

By the time we finished dinner, it was late. I was led off to the guest house, beautifully prepared for me. Two fragrant plumeria trees had even been planted on either side that day to honor my arrival. Gail and I hugged again and said our good nights. Alone in the guest house, I unpacked, peeking into corners and cabinets. Among other things, I saw about fifty books that Gail, inspired by my intention to write a book about healing and health, had decided I should look at. I was touched to see that her all-embracing desire to help was already at work.

The night was lovely. Thoughts of snowdrifts in Connecticut were literally thousands of miles away. After a shower to wash off the day, I flopped into bed. The caressing sounds of the Pacific entered though the cottage's windows, lulling me rhythmically to sleep.

Morning brought an array of new, unfamiliar sounds. Someone was high up on a palm tree chopping down coconuts, and the *thwack* of a machete was competing with the ocean's leonine roar. Throwing on shorts and a tee shirt, I hauled myself over to the house. There I was greeted by Waldo, the house mascot, and the promise of Gail's hemp pancakes. "Marijuana," she called them, amusingly if inaccurately. Raymie was already gone. She'd set up breakfast on the porch, where we leisurely devoured the food and Hawaiian Kona coffee, catching up on intervening months of our journey to be well.

Gail was evasive about herself. That worried me, though I didn't want to push. I began to discover that she had plans for me. Most importantly, she wanted me to see the doctor treating her in Honolulu, a Dr. Lam. We discussed him briefly, and I told her I'd think it over.

In addition to something called the Dermatron, which Dr. Lam used, Gail 's treatment program made use of three other machines. Two of them, each geared to arrest cancer growth by way of vibrational work, were definitely out of the mainstream. One was called the Beam Ray; the other, a molecule enhancer, was used to increase the voltage of the cells. The third device, the regulation thermography machine, was more well-known, although still considered alternative. She flew over to California periodically to be checked by one of the world experts in the field of dynamic regulation thermography.

She was dedicated to her program, which also included a diet of alkaline foods, regular colonics, and the self-treatment of coffee enemas. The family refrigerator was packed with tablets, green drinks, alkalizing fizzes, nuts, seeds, grains, and a veritable pharmacopoeia of natural, organic foodstuffs. She was widely read in the field of health and alternative treatments. But she never forced her ideas on me, only suggested, say, that some enzyme or "new" seaweed would be a great thing to include in my diet. I tried to be similarly respectful, though I remained worried that her condition had worsened. In matters of giving support to friends, I've learned, it's important to be sensitive to their beliefs. Challenge can be unhelpful, even if you are suspect of their approach. It's always dangerous and unfair to encroach on hope.

Over the next days, I set up my schedule. I worked in my cottage all morning, still figuring out what I wanted to say. Was my book to be a memoir, a guide, a combination of both? I wasn't yet sure, so I just wrote about all my experiences including my take on Yale, the clinic, and the doctors I'd met. There were also random scribblings about midnight wake-ups while going through chemo, thoughts about my life, reflections on reactions I'd had. It was still way too large and miscellaneous, but it was a start. I found it both challenging and rewarding to work on figuring out what the actual benefits of my journey had been to me in the deepest sense. When I needed a break, I perused the library of books Gail had left for me. Some were helpful, though others were so far out they didn't seem relevant to me.

Gail was a working woman: the powerhouse and creative force, I surmised, in the design company she owned with her husband, Miller and Miller. Her own home décor told me how gifted she was as a designer-decorator. The house had been the manager's residence of an old sugar plantation; it was built in wood, with cedar stairs, floors and banisters that were highly polished but simple. The furnishings were mostly rattan or teak, imported from Indonesia and making an elegant showcase for Gail's design style. Antique objects and furniture from Asia and lovely contemporary prints, as well as original art by the late Hawaiian artist John Kelly, accented the house. The kitchen had large black and white squares on the floor and all the cabinets holding china and pots and pans were wood with glass doors, light and airy. Ceiling fans were everywhere, cooling the house, which was positioned to give it the benefit of fragrant cross breezes.

Waldo, the yellow Lab and mascot, was always curious. Bigglesworth, a marmalade cat that was there to be his playmate, sinuously crept around the porch fencing. Their colors as a pair were in perfect synch, either a decorating touch or a good day at the animal rescue center. Gail found great joy in her flowers and arrangements, so orchids and exotic Birds of Paradise arrangements adorned the house. Simple but chic print cushions provided touches of color, a counterpoint to the all-white upholstery of everything else. There was a huge TV, but no actual TV service. The TV was exclusively used for videos, as Gail deplored the violence of television programming.

Each day before Gail left for work, we'd walk across the road—a quiet highway—to reach Gail's special band of beach and ocean. There she knew the currents and the tilt of the sand banks, so we'd be safe and private. She always had her eye on me, especially as we had to climb some rocks to get there. But the minute we arrived, she became a sun goddess, in her natural element swimming and sunning. She adored both; she would just lay there in bliss, the great importance of this experience to her sense of well-being totally obvious. This was her way of relaxing, letting go and loving nature.

About the third day of my visit, Gail again mentioned Dr. Lam and how much she believed he could help me. He was a Hawaiian of Chinese extraction, she explained, who graduated from Case-Western Reserve medical school but had switched from conventional, allopathic practice to practicing as a homeopathic doctor. In particular, he used a technique based on electo-acupuncture, involving the Dermatron machine I mentioned earlier, to both diagnose and treat. He believed that when the correct homeopathic remedy was placed in the patient's hands, then tested, their electrical readings would improve; when removed, those 'good' readings would deteriorate. When the most useful remedies had been selected, the patient would take them and self-inject subcutaneously and the body would react.

Gail's almost messianic belief in Dr. Lam was a bit disconcerting. This was especially true since her condition, about which she was always a bit guarded, had deteriorated under his care, prompting her visit to the Paracelsus Clinic. She still absolutely refused any chemo-therapy or radiation, so he was treating her only with electro-acu-puncture.

I was still self-injecting with the mistletoe ampoules, religiously following the clinic's regime. With that, and having experienced chemo, I wasn't thrilled by taking on more needles, even if the treatment was homeopathic. As I told Gail, I was feeling much better, but it worried me not to have regained my former energy levels. Home-opathy is considered safe (in fact, many consider it useless) and I knew enough to believe it certainly wouldn't hurt me. In addition, my curiosity about treatments designed to heal rather than just remove symptoms was boundless. So I finally agreed to make an appointment with the doctor. I thought it might help with the remaining toxins in the body. As she wanted it so much for me, I gave in.

Hawaiians use small planes as we would use trains or the subway, thinking nothing of going over to another of the islands for a few hours or the day. I took the commuter plane back to Oahu with Gail. My appointment was first—she had errands to do before her own session. She pointed me in the right direction with typically vague Hawaiian navigation and I soon found myself in front of a rather nondescript, slightly shabby building of about five stories high. Finding the elevator, I ascended to the third floor, then negotiated a few twists and turns in a hallway until I came to Dr. Lam's office. On entering, I heard Christian music blaring, extolling Jesus. I remembered Gail saying that hearing that same music when she entered the office for the first time had convinced her that God had led her to Dr. Lam. Being something of a New York cynic, I wasn't waiting for the Second Coming just then, but I was undeniably fascinated.

I announced myself and sat in the crowded waiting room. Those of us waiting all turned our heads in unison as the door swung open. In strode a tall, elderly, very elegant Chinese man wearing a lab coat and Bass Weejuns, shined to a high brilliance. He disappeared into the inner sanctum, left the office again after a few minutes, then returned after a short absence. Following a substantial wait, my turn rolled around and I went into his office, a large sunny room with lots of equipment, including a large machine with numerous attachments. This was the Dermatron, switched on and humming.

The testing procedure was arcane, totally foreign from any American experience I'd had. In one hand, I would hold a homeopathic tincture; in the other, I held a contraption like one half of a skipping rope, made of metal and attached to the Dermatron. I ended up with about six remedies. The number jarred me, momentarily undermining my faith in all my detox work to date. However, Gail later allowed that this was nothing compared to what some came away with. The clinic had all of the supplies I needed, so I left prepared. They included instructions which prescribed drinking 20 or more glasses of water after the first shot. This would help expel the toxins and prevent them from re-establishing themselves, according to homeopathic principles. They also warned of flu-like symptoms that might arise as the toxins were expelled. I took my parcel, paid, and wondered if I was being really smart or a total idiot.

By the time I was finished and sitting with my brown paper package, Gail had finished her appointment. As we left for the airport, she was eager to have my impressions. I wasn't exactly sure what to say. The conditions Dr. Lam had diagnosed, including toxoplasmosis caught from cats, had not been picked up by the clinic. For the moment, I concluded that Dr. Lam and Dr. Rau were working on two essentially different issues. Lam focused on his 'mother tinctures' to pick up on small, specific areas of inflammation or bacterial disturbance, whereas Dr. Rau was focusing on the entire body. It turned out that a couple of Dr. Lam's conclusions were incorrect, but as I had known, the treatment did me no harm.

The experience with the Dermatron brought a new insight as well. I was beginning to laugh at myself a little, realizing I had become a doctor junkie and it was time to stop. On the other hand, my curiosity prompted explorations that might unfold valuable information others didn't yet have. I was entirely open to the idea that there were special people outside the conventional mold of medical care who might offer interesting possibilities for improvements in health.

I now think that by trying all these unconventional techniques, Gail and I were attempting to fence in our raw fear. It was natural to want to be able to beat our cancer with just 'natural' therapies, given how much damage is done to the body by chemo and radiation. But as I only realized later, Gail's condition was much more serious than she let on. We were each assuming full responsibility for our health and healing, but our approaches were quite different. I had hated chemo but had fully submitted to the protocol designed by Dr. Schwartz. To my mind, he was brilliant and informed in gynecological cancers, and I wanted the benefit of his expertise. Gail had taken a different path. She bore the additional burden of having lost her sister to breast cancer a few years before, another threat to her existence. Though her parents lived on Maui, clearly the most important person in her life was her son, Raymond, physically a stunningly handsome combination of Raymie and Gail.

In the cottage each morning, I continued dipping into Gail's library in moments of spare time. Mostly I concentrated on writing about my experiences at the clinic and all that preceded them, trying to truthfully and deeply mine where I was right now, after what I hoped was the worst. I was working to establish a writer's habits, carving out a special time each day to write. The physical discipline came easily and some words always came out. I tried not to worry too much about the content, but rather to just let them flow.

We often had lunch together, but she went to work most days, visiting the Miller and Miller office and furniture warehouse in Lihue and island-hopping to see clients. John called me quite often during this time and I found that his calls made me feel happy and upbeat. He had never been to Hawaii, so I described the island for him. All the bird life and flora for which Kauai is known interested him as he has always loved nature, birds, animals and anything to do with their habitat.

Gail and I would walk for an hour or so most days. The conversation usually revolved around the same subjects: the weather, the "flipper" which replaced my front tooth, her son Raymond and my relationship with John. She liked the sound of him and loved his voice on the telephone. She wanted to meet him, offering the cottage to us if he wanted to be part of any next visit. That sounded like a nice idea to me. Perpetually romantic but a realist as well, Gail wanted me to be with someone special, and so, I realized, did I both want and need that very much.

One morning she suggested we go north on Kauai, to the posh part of the island. We took my Jeep and I drove while she gave the directions. Princeville, where we were headed, is quite different than Waimea. The houses up country have a different feel; many are centered on the ocean, but a little away off, with views of waterfalls and jungle type growth. We had planned a walk so I'd see the famous Napali Coast and get a better view of Nihau, the island privately owned by the Robinson family.

Upon arriving in Princeville, we did a quick scan of some of the fancy houses and headed to Ke'e Beach, where the eleven mile Napali Coast trail begins. Given our costumes and the notorious rockiness of the trail, we must have been quite an eye-catching pair, both touching and hilarious. Gail was wearing her South Sea pearl necklace, all her silver bracelets (a trademark of hers), a mini skirt and Nike backless shoes with no tread. I was in shorts and ballerina shoes with no tread and no ankle support. Gail later pointed out that I was toothless in front; I often didn't put in the plate or "flipper," as I found it so uncomfortable. I also had my water bottle hanging around my waist, using an old Hermes scarf as a belt. This picture of the two of us is lost to posterity as we didn't have a camera. Looking out at Nihau and intoxicated by the beauty of the craggy walk, I turned to Gail and said, "Let's say a prayer and hope our children and grandchildren can see this."

We hadn't planned to walk the entire eleven miles of the Kalalau trail, which is rocky and rigorous. But we talked and laughed as we went, making it feel much like the first walk we took together in Switzerland, high above the clinic's village, when we had felt so much warmth and affection for each other. One properly shod and well-attired hiker looked at us with amusement, telling us we were the best dressed hikers she'd seen that day. I gave her a huge toothless smile in thanks as we continued on in the other direction.

It had been a funny, wonderful day. The beauty and calm were never to be forgotten, nor the feeling of being transported to a different realm where woes don't exist. Tired by the day and the drive back, we cracked open a bottle of red wine back home. Sitting on the swinging sofa on the front porch, we talked about our plans and listened to the ocean. My own to-do list included continuing to work toward greater clarity of mind, a process I couldn't rush. You can't legislate clear thinking after cancer, I had learned, but I knew that despite whatever was still unclear, I was getting someplace. Writing the book and being with Gail had helped tremendously. Her love and openness, and our mutual understanding, were hugely important at this juncture.

I would be leaving a few days later. Knowing that Gail faced more medical challenges than I did, I felt concerned about her. When I asked to hear more about her plans, she spoke of treatment with a Munich doctor who harvested your cancer cells and made a vaccine. I knew she was also anxious to get to California to see her doctor there. I continued to have a feeling that things were not going well. But whatever the reason was for keeping it to herself, I didn't feel I could, or should, either intervene or ask too much.

On the morning of my departure, I hauled my bags out of my delightful cottage, took a last sniff of the now-blooming plumeria trees, and had a quick breakfast with Gail. A look in her eye worried me again—one of fearfulness, I thought. I was reassured to know that she had many friends and supporters on the island, most notably a German woman named Gabriella. She thought very highly of this neighbor. Gabriella wasn't always on Kauai; it transpired that in the winter, Gabriella lived in the same community I now inhabit in Florida.

Later, Gabriella filled in many of the blanks regarding Gail's last months. I gave Gail the best pep talk I could, suggesting she return to the clinic if she was worried, telling her I was there for her, and reminding her that I'd come to see her the moment she let me know I was needed.

Gail was not good at good-byes. I am better, most of the time. Tears in her eyes, she handed me a care package of Hawaiian pineapple marmalade for John and some plumeria perfume for me. As I got into the Jeep I felt a deep, spirit-level gratitude for my host and hostess. They had made me feel welcome, as if family. While with them, I had had few worries and enjoyed a most precious commodity: unbounded time to sit, relax, walk, read and work. I had benefited from the shared time with someone whose experience with serious illness was similar to mine, and who understood the kind of fears and pressure healthy people may not understand. Gail was perceptive and had read my thoughts, eliciting insights that I hadn't figured out yet on my own. John's frequent calls added to my feeling of being cared for. Luggage and me aboard, I turned on the Jeep's ignition, waved until all were out of sight, and headed for the third palm tree on the right. My flight was ready and waiting to return me and my dreams to New York.

21

Diamond Head

But let there be spaces in your togetherness.

— KAHLIL GIBRAN

More isn't always more. Back in the East, after Hawaii, it was clear my life was smaller, less active on the outside. Yet it was busy and growing on the inside. The quest for greater awareness and staying rooted in the present moment was being actively practiced, sometimes just by sitting quietly observing myself observe myself. If Dr. Rau's theory of seasons was right, I felt that I might be on my way to achieving those qualities which the winter season represents. I had been stuck for about forty years, not having experienced them and was finally finding and enjoying the warmth of family associated with that season although often outside of "official" familial channels. My, how we can create our own kith and kin!

I no longer had an apartment of my own in the city. But close friends, Audrey and Henry Koehler, had a tiny but charming apartment in the East 70s which they weren't really using. They rented it to me for a song, creating a perfect domicile for my forays into New York. It brought me back to my old neighborhood; the apartment was as well-appointed and easy on the eyes as I could possibly want with Henry's paintings and art throughout and Audrey's decor. Good things seemed to be falling in my lap. The seeming ease of those dividends, I attributed to the changes in energy and new thinking.

All of a sudden, it was May and I was in the middle of rehearsals for a group performance to celebrate the Centennial for my club in New York, the Colony Club. I was slated to perform a couple of solo numbers. Kitty Carlisle Hart, a longtime member—then in her nineties but still going strong—was a cast member, too. In fact, the performers were drawn only from the club's members, except for the accompanist and the occasional husband, if he could sing.

In the weeks before the event, Marianne Challis worked me as hard as I ever had worked. Chris Marlowe and I rehearsed and rehearsed the arrangements. One of my favorite songs was "Let's Do It" by Cole Porter. It gave me an opportunity to add my own lyrics in the final verses, using the names of celebrities of the time, who were fun to send up. My practice was revealing significant improvements in vocal flexibility due to the decrease of tension in my jaw and neck, my two former nemeses. The detoxes and other work I had done were, no doubt, the cause of this release of vocal power and ease. It was a happy surprise for Chris, Marianne and me. I was ready to go–a great feeling that sometimes reduced me to tears of relief and wonderment. Feeling the changes only reinforced the desire to stick to my program of diet, supplements, yoga and spiritual Eurythmy exercises.

Much of my thinking was about and around John. I would often call from Audrey and Henry's in the late afternoon, having returned from the day's activities, to see if he wanted to have dinner. I missed him and our surroundings in the old apartment. Often, he was free and we would meet up; John always game to go out to dinner. We are both total New Yorkers, and New Yorkers love to dine out—hence the 40,000 restaurants or more in the city.

As I spent these days and weeks, often on my own in my solitary space, it reminded me that two big aspects of my personality continued to be stumbling blocks, needing to be faced: pride and perfectionism. In the past, my pride had influenced too much of my behavior, such as being unable to admit that I was wrong, fighting on, trying to wriggle out of not being right about something, anything. Perfectionism, I realized, was exhausting and lethal. Besides, perfect doesn't exist and the pillows don't always need to be perfectly plumped! I still work against the two pernicious "P"s.

A performer can feel audience receptivity; a receptive crowd can draw out a more relaxed performance, where you stop thinking about breathing or lyrics and just *flow*. The night of my performance at the Club, that's what happened for the first time ever in my singing. The show was a big success and the audience loved my slightly wicked version of "Let's Do It."

John was in the audience. Kitty, one of the great show business veterans, made a special point of coming to congratulate me on my performance. Earlier in the evening, during drinks upstairs, she had asked me about John. Was he single? What did he do? Why, "for heaven's sake," had we divorced? Raising her diamond-studded lorgnette to peer into my eyes, she said "What is wrong with you? He is a great guy?" The next day, I ran into another fellow club member who swore she and John had shared the same sandbox as kids. "I was watching John watching you. He's still in love with you," she said before she smiled, gave me a hug and dashed off to lunch.

The summer came and went. I was spending a lot of time in the country. I drove up to see Philippa, "her" John and my granddaughter Miranda. I had a lot of dinners with friends locally, sometimes staying over in "my room" with the Kinsolvings. Susan and I watched reruns of "The Sopranos," which we had never seen before and found hysterically funny. It had been a good summer for me; I was happy.

John and I also went to Scotland for a visit, during which Anastasia and Stefan came up for a long weekend. They were well, and both of them loved and understood the draw of life in the Scottish countryside. At Downey Park house, our rental, it stayed light until about ten at night during the summer—it's that far north. John would walk down to the river after dinner, all dolled up in his waders and jacket, with his rod and flies hanging off his vest. He would try for a salmon or sea trout, and was often successful. On previous visits, I had discovered the joy of catching and smoking your own salmon. You can choose the 'smoke,' light, heavy, unflavored or natural. Delicious!

Our relationship was growing again. It deepened as we revisited places where we had both been happy and engaged, enjoying the surroundings, Scottish friends, and just being together.

As I've explained earlier, trust had been difficult for me since childhood, especially with regards to men. Now, those insecurities were affecting me less and less It was finally sinking in that John Horn was about the most trustworthy, loyal, loveable guy on the planet. A handshake was his bond, as was his word. I realized, too, that he has amazing insights into people and their essential character. Maybe his years of judging stocks quickly, needing to make snap decisions, formed some of that ability, or it was simply an intuitive gift.

That said, he could say "no" before you felt he'd heard what you had to say. We were both strong and stubborn in our own ways. Neither of us liked giving in. It had taken me time to realize his sometimes gruff responses were a mask for great sweetness. He loved beauty, not only in nature and gardening but in art and objects—I'd always been impressed by his ability to drop into an antique shop and return with some beautiful piece of carved wood or small object; He is a romantic at heart. Above all, many of his decisions are based on 'getting a kick out of' something, a delightful quality. I don't mean drugs or alcohol, though he loves his wines; he just has a willingness to embrace that which brings fun, life, and joy. Now, I was realizing again how much I valued his sense of fun, and how much I had missed the kindness in his eyes.

I was seeing that relationships have moods, that they may be better in one place than another or on one day than another. I saw more deeply than before that there's a yin and yang to the rhythm of them, and that letting things be is often the best medicine. I was finding my own balance. I was often reminded that we humans live within a spiritual context; it's best to remember that and leave the superficialities in the chamber marked "less important Items." What I may not like in myself is just a small part of who or what I am; the same applies to everyone else. I learned to trust that truth more deeply that summer.

Time passed. I was in my house in Litchfield County doing the same things: working on my book, working on myself, still exploring those spaces inside my psyche. In a bittersweet moment that reminded me how far I'd come, I turned in the old Audi, my teacher and cicerone. Mice had invaded it over the winter. It had also failed going up a snowy hill one evening, which had left me anxious about driving it. My old friend had served me well during a very difficult and challenging period in my life, but it was time to move on. I chose a smaller, slightly less powerful replacement that fitted where I was now.

It was time to go back to see Gail. We needed to check in with each other. When I called, the same conditions applied—I was told to make my reservations and that she would be waiting for me. There was something odd, a tone in her voice when we spoke, that I didn't like the sound of, but I wasn't sure.

She suggested I bring John if he'd like to come. She was funny: had clearly decided it would be good for him to be there, and was pushing for my relationship with him to work this time around. I asked him if he'd like to go to Kauai, explaining the situation. Always sensitive, he arranged his flights so I could be there a few days on my own before he arrived, giving Gail and me a chance to visit without distractions.

Suddenly it was February and I was back, like a homing pigeon, in the familiar cottage. My plumeria trees had grown a lot and were in bloom. Gail and I were so happy to be reunited. She was busy: her son Raymond was coming for a visit, things did not seem easy between her and Raymie, and I sensed that the business too was having difficulties. She seemed to be doubling up on her self-treatments with her machines at home, which gave me grave doubts about the state of her health. Nevertheless, she opened her heart and house as before.

I had a follow-up appointment with Dr. Lam at which I was pronounced "all clear." About five days into the visit, I drove in to pick up John. Gail treated him as if he was one of her oldest, dearest friends. We had a glass of wine, talked on the front verandah for a while, then headed off to the cottage for the night. We were cozy and happy to be reunited, and I went to sleep grateful for this wonderful guy who had flown almost half way around the world to be with his former wife. By my side was someone I had worked to forgive, as he had figured out forgiveness in his own way. We were there, in the present moment, to do as we wished, as if with a clean slate.

Gail waved us off to explore the islands on our own. One day, we went up to Princeville and stayed overnight at the fancy hotel there. Back in Waimea, on another night, we went to a place called the Wranglers with Raymie and Gail to hear the ukuleles and singing— the most indigenous, Hawaiian cultural event on that part of the island other than hula lessons.

I wanted John to see Honolulu, one of the world's most cosmopolitan cities and a real gateway to the Far East. We wandered the city during the day and ate dinner on Gail's recommendation at the best hotel on Diamond Head. Our table was in the hotel's outdoor restaurant, a rustic place with wooden floors and tables set around a big bar in the middle. I remember sitting there, both of us contemplative, waiting for a glass of wine or the menu or the waiter. Underneath that surface, however, there was something else going on. It wasn't as if I felt like a twenty-year-old, with all the excitement of starting out, having a man 'pop the question' or contemplating an entire life together with children and choices and careers. We'd done that, for the most part. What we didn't have was a partnership together, a total commitment or day–to-day intimacy.

John had horn rimmed glasses then, which made him look quite striking. In fact, another diner came over to the table and wanted to know who he was. "You look so distinguished," said she, making us both laugh.

Shortly after that moment, John reached for my hand. "I think we should get back together," he said. I held my breath for a few seconds, squeezed his hand back, and nodded in assent.

It felt tremendously right, this bond that had been slowly rebuilding itself over the past year and a half. In so many ways, we were very different, yet I realized that the deep underlying respect and love we had for each other had only wobbled during that rough time. Then it had righted itself, like one of those toys you can push yet never quite knock over. The past seemed healed; there we were, ready to try again. I'd found him again, in part because I'd found myself. My illness had begun a journey that had brought me full circle through the illness, in a profound way; I'd finally met my womanhood full on. John was my rock. I loved him and he loved me. I knew that I could trust him and more importantly, I knew that I could trust myself.

We got back to Kauai and while we weren't emailing folks at home the news, I told Gail. Naturally, she was thrilled, knowing she played a part in all of it, and provided a good bottle of champagne on our last night. Back in Connecticut, I made a call to the local minister in Washington Depot, where there is a sweet, small Episcopal church we both liked. When I got Bob Fix, the minister, on the telephone and recounted our history, there was a deafening silence on the line for a moment. Then Bob tactfully explained that it would be impossible for him to marry us in the church. We'd used up our free passes, so to speak, each having been married twice before in the Episcopal church. Instead, he suggested a Justice of the Peace in the nearby town of Litchfield. I had to smile. Obviously not everyone would see our re-marriage as quite the natural thing that we did.

Come December, we went to the town hall in the town of Litch-field, armed with "his and hers" divorce decrees and birth certificates. The blue-rinsed lady in the marriages, births and deaths department, who might have emerged straight from a Norman Rockwell painting, came to the front desk as we waved our papers. It took her a second to register what she saw in them, the same name and address on each document. Then, canny New Englander that she was, she smiled, took the papers and got to work, her neat, pink nails tapping away at our license on an electric typewriter, her blue eyes twinkling.

Neither John nor I can remember the exact date although we both remember our first wedding date in May. It was about a week before Christmas. I spent the night before with him at his farm. This time there was no bridal superstition about not being glimpsed by the groom before the wedding. Grey northern Connecticut skies loomed in the morning; eleven o'clock was the appointed time. I hadn't really planned what to wear. I rooted around in my former closet and found a festive red skirt. I had checked my jewelry box earlier and found my old wedding ring, patiently waiting to be put to use. John looked very good in his grey country flannels. He even put on a tie for the occasion, as we were planning to celebrate with lunch at a nearby inn.

The service was short, but tender in its own way. I think even the judge was touched. We were only there for a few minutes. We said our vows, John holding my hand tightly, then we kissed, thanked the judge, and left to have our wedding lunch. That night, Isabel and Winston Fowlkes gave us a small dinner. The dearest of "usual suspects" appeared, including William and Susan Kinsolving and Drika and Alex Purvis. Neither my girls nor John's sons attended; we had the fancy wedding the previous time and it didn't feel necessary. But all the children seemed very pleased. My daughters had always been very fond of John, and I am sure they were relieved to see me settled.

As we headed back to the farm, I knew that we were picking up where we left off years before, and I liked it. We belonged together. I also was pretty sure it wouldn't always be easy, yet stayed positive that it was right. It would be good, I knew, never perfect, but always interesting, and well worth the doing of it again.

Part of my joy stemmed from understanding that I was in a very different place than I had been before my cancer diagnosis. The illness itself and the long journey it initiated had transformed me. I had cleaned up much if not all of my unfinished emotional business—all, I think, is impossible. I had become an elder, gaining wisdom and a richer approach to living, as well as a stronger sense of my own identity. My remarriage to John was just one outward sign of many new directions emerging from the "little touch of cancer" that had made me well.

Epilogue

We are the choices we have made.

— MERYL STREEP

John and I settled in fairly easily from the beginning. The learning curve was not so steep the second time; John's rock-solid stability became my linchpin. Being settled, truly settled, in a loving relationship based on trust has been a springboard towards a general contentment I have never experienced before. He is energized by my desire to learn and to do, while I have become more relaxed and calm.

Six months after we had exchanged vows, we were back in Scotland and I came across an advertisement for a charming old castle in a magazine. Or, rather, the ad was for its remains, now converted to a livable house but with towers, ancient walls and a big garden remaining. When John asked what I was looking at, I passed over the magazine. "Let's go and see it," he said. It surprised me, but I called and made the appointment.

From the moment we approached—through two tall, acorn-shaped stone pillars and gates attached to ruined towers—something special happened. It was akin to a Brigadoon moment. We instantly fell madly in love with the Craig, so reduced in size from wars, explosions and fires and moats collapsing. We had to be there, experience this historic and very quirky house for ourselves, and attach a piece of our own history to it. Four days later, our bid was accepted. The experience was a total departure from anything we'd done before. I guess that it was proof of the trust we had in each other, as well as of the possibilities of new beginnings at any stage of life.

I have often thought about the hyperthermia session in Switzerland when I had a vision of John and I being together and building a beautiful, big garden. What I envisioned was just like the one at the Craig. I must wonder if I knew more than I knew that I knew. The Scots would call that 'canny', and I believe it was. The Craig continues to delight and give pleasure to us and to our friends and family. We have loved fixing it up, recreating some of its former glories, giving the house a legacy from us for posterity. We have even enjoyed having a ghost for the first time. There have been several sightings of the "green lady," but not by me.

In Scotland and back in America, my book progressed. Like many first-time authors, I found the process much slower than I expected, the task not just of writing but equally of self-reflection. My predisposition to hoard and rip any article on medicine I felt worthy of inclusion in the book became a joke. As my folders and files stacked up, John has mused that we might have to add a room. All the paper reminded him of the Collyer Brothers in New York City, famous hoarders. I reassure myself with the thought that all of the material that has not made it into the book can be used on my website, blog, in workshops and in other books.

I continue to approach my life knowing that I am a work in progress. Part of the reason I am here, I believe, is to continue to learn and to grow as a person. With that among other things in mind, I decided to return to school and take some courses a few months after our remarriage. It has been a joy to be back at school, especially given the improvement in my concentration and in the satisfaction of learning itself with classroom discipline and deadlines. John has been amused and delighted by my efforts, and the periodic overnight break while I am at school has proved positive for two semi-loners. I hope to fulfill my long-postponed goal of acquiring my Bachelor of Arts degree before the age of 90.

Physically, I am well—indeed, better than ever before. The knowledge that a recurrence of my cancer is possible exercises a certain control over my life, ensuring that I don't veer too far off my path. Navigating cancer with all its twists and turns added measurable steel to my spine; the desire to live strengthened my will; my understanding that negative emotion and stress can affect my health right at the cellular level reminds me to enjoy each day—to live it as fully as possible and with gratitude.

Though it took some time, I finally stopped searching out every doctor or practitioner's office who sounded the slightest bit interesting. (Still, I shamelessly admit a mini-career as a physicians' "groupie.") In the midst of that quest, I sometimes felt like a pre-med student wildly taking notes and asking questions; at other times, I wondered if I was simply another neurotic woman being self-indulgent. I can see now that I was still coping with the shock of having had cancer. I'm grateful that each mentor has taught me something, helping me find and place another piece into the jigsaw puzzle of my life. I had a good laugh one day when I revisited an old contacts list and found fourteen dentists listed. Having pulled the plug on collecting doctors, I have culled and kept only what works best.

Though I have never for a moment regretted the dental work recommended by Dr. Rau, my dental odyssey has been a long and sometimes odd journey. By 2004 or so, the "flipper" that replaced my front tooth had begun to annoy me past the point of tolerance, reaching nightmare status. It was so irritating that I sometimes left it out in public, even going out to restaurants without it. Gail came up with what I hoped would be a permanent answer, so I made one more short trip to Hawaii to see a dentist there. I loved the work he did on replacing my front tooth, though the replacement has since been replaced itself, with a titanium implant.

While I remained healthy, Gail did not fare so well. She called one day in 2007 to say that she was going to Munich to see a doctor, the one who would create a vaccine through harvesting the patient's own cancer cells. She asked if I'd meet her there and stay with her for a few days while she decided whether or not to go ahead with this rigorous, expensive treatment. Of course, I would and did. As soon as I arrived in Munich, I joined her for dinner at a bistro near the hotel. She was as loving as ever, but things were definitely not good. She and Raymie had parted, and she had undergone a double mastectomy. I knew her situation was serious. I invited her to stay with us in Scotland during the 'off days' from Munich if she decided to go forward. She decided to stay in London, where the plane service was better, instead, but Gail and her beloved son Raymond came to visit us for Christmas at the Craig in the middle of her treatment. She found the gravestones of Scottish ancestors while handsome Raymond charmed the local lassies. It would be the last time we saw each other. Although I didn't know that yet, I remember cherishing every moment of a lovely visit with my funny, lovely friend and feeling that she did the same.

Gail deteriorated very quickly once she returned to Hawaii, and died four years ago, in 2009. Her friend Gabriella, who as I've mentioned lives in the same community I do during the winter, helped her at the end of her life. I am grateful that Gabriella has shared the details of that time with me. I grieve deeply for the loss of this wonderful person and spirit. I wonder sometimes if embracing conventional as well as complementary treatment, as I did, would have made a difference for her. Yet her decisions about this came from within; she thought she was making the best possible choices for herself, and though I disagreed, I am grateful to have been there to support her. I have heard that her son Raymond has married and become a father. I can only imagine how much she would have adored a grandchild. I hope very much that her grandchild is lucky enough to be something like Gail.

I myself now have three grandchildren: Miranda, Iona and Alexander. They are among my greatest joys. I am dedicated to helping in any way to further their progress as well-rounded and valuable citizens who will be heading into a very challenging world.

Early this year, on a lark, I entered the Ms. Senior Florida pageant—and won it, winning the talent portion as well. I felt all those scales and lessons had paid off, and remembered Steven Forrest's comment that my most important work would be as an elder. This book is launching a website dedicated to healthy aging for the over-forties, and frivolous as the pageant seems in some ways (I have been threatening to write a comic novel about it), it is an affirmation of the vibrancy and dynamism of older women. So I feel a pattern in all these choices—reassuring, after many years of living and feeling that things didn't quite connect.

If my story conveys a message, I hope it is this. First, that there are tremendous possibilities for transformation residing under the cover of serious illness. Second, and closely related, that regaining mastery of one's health sometimes requires gaining mastery over one's biography. It also requires hard work and commitment. I don't hate, or even really regret, my cancer. I believe that it has been my ally, my friend. Without it, I would not have arrived at the place I find myself in now: a place where I understand life and its complexities more fully, have forgiven myself and others more truthfully, appreciate the power and joy of living in the present and look forward to the future with eagerness and joy.

.

Betsy's Toolbox

To me, old age is always fifteen years older than
I am.

— BERNARD BARUCH

This book shares the pivotal moments of the journey toward wellness
that began with my cancer diagnosis. Yet optimal well-being is built
not just from diagnoses, consults and treatments, but also from smaller,
more habitual, less dramatic actions that are the stuff of everyday life.
The following is a review of the elements that are part of my daily
routine. Together, I believe they keep me fit and in optimal health.
They include the obligatory elements like diet and physical exercise,
working on psycho-emotional well-being, and a spiritual practice—
the most difficult part of my "toolbox" to describe, yet still essential.

In sharing my own strategies, I hope not just to make helpful suggestions but also to inspire you to assess and perhaps tweak your own
wellness "toolbox." Clearly, what's below is a personal, eclectic perspective. As I have mentioned in the book, there is no "one size fits
all" approach; neither in any way is this an attempt to make a diagnosis or to suggest that a strategy that works for me will work for you.
Any program you adopt should be checked with your own physician
or medical advisor, as well as with your own instinct about what fits
you best.

My website, www.betsyhorn.com, discusses (or will discuss) all of
these subjects in greater detail, offering many free resources and

information as well as links (in the wellness store) to some of the products discussed below. Please visit me there for more help with issues listed in this Toolbox, as well as subjects beyond its scope.

As you'll see, my personal program involves many elements. I have put them in alphabetical order to avoid the overlaps that would arise in trying to replicate my actual daily routine. Where I have found a particular product or brand to be especially excellent, I mention it below and many, not all, can be found and purchased in my wellness store. I receive no remuneration for these references, for which links are provided on my website. I note them simply for whatever assistance they may provide to you.

Even once you have developed a comfortable routine, circumstances may prompt you to make changes as new issues and situations develop. As we age, there will always be challenges and new concerns. Even a strategy that worked ideally for many years may need adjusting over time. I have been working for years on issues such as my autonomic nervous system, for example. Now, maintaining balance physically and working on my bone health have emerged as additional and key components of my fitness routine. As my personal relationships change, so must my ways of dealing with them. In that sense, this "toolbox" is always a work in progress, as your own should be as well.

Alkalinity: As discussed in the book, keeping the body alkaline is an important part of maintaining health and avoiding disease. My diet is largely plant based with plenty of alkaline veggies, and when consuming animal protein, my portion is about the size of my palm (which is medium sized).

Aromatherapy Oils: I keep an arsenal of good, essential oils wherever I am. I especially like the oils from a company called Young Living. They offer an excellent array, and all of their oils are certified organic and approved for internal as well as external use.

Either just before or just after my morning meditation, while I am still in bed, I rub my feet and lower legs with essential oils (Dr. Haushcka's Rosemary Leg and Arm Toner) to assist circulation. At the same time, I stretch out my toes and ankles, doing a few ankle rotations, and pull my toes which can curl and tighten up overnight. When traveling, I take a small bottle of lavender oil or spray to create my own little universe, especially on a crowded plane. I'll often put a few drops of peppermint oil on my tongue before going out to a meal to protect against indigestion or contamination in food—this oil is good for inducing warmth and thought to be an anti-microbial barrier. If you plan to try this, check any oils you buy carefully to make sure they are certified for internal use.

Breathing. I believe that a practice of diaphragmatic breathing is elemental in safeguarding the body's heath. Most of us breathe in a hurried, shallow fashion. Moreover, our natural breathing abilities and rhythms become less efficient as we age; most of us use less than a fifth of the lung capacity available. Though the diaphragm is an involuntary muscle and breathing is mostly automatic, we can decide when and how we want to take a breath. When we make it a habit to breathe deeply and fully, we oxygenate and clean the tissues—a stellar result for a simple habit. "Because we usually take breathing for granted, we tend not to realize the harmful effects faulty breathing can have on us, or the freedom we can gain by improving how we breathe," says Jessica Wolf, creator of *The Art of Breathing Rib Animation* DVD and teacher of the Alexander Technique at Yale Drama School.

In addition to its physical benefits, conscious breathing calms the mind, slows the heart, lessens anxiety and panic, and helps us to stay relaxed and in the present moment.

My morning process upon waking begins with at least 6 good deep breaths, which are helpful in reducing cortisol levels, which may be high in the morning. I let the breath come as it needs to and focus on the exhale. Exhaling is the most important part of the breath, as it removes carbon dioxide from the cells. I try to be conscious of my breathing throughout the day and find myself more relaxed at the end of the day, if I have been aware of my breath.

Chiropractic: Nancy Lasak, my chiropractor, has kept me and my spine flexible and out of pain. There is a lot to be said for a 'bones' doctor, as they can address tightness in the muscles as well as spinal imbalance. A good treatment releases tension and increases flexibility, both helpful in a culture where many of us sit at a desk—or lean over a portable device—for many hours a day. Chiropractors are knowledgeable about nutrition and have as many if not more hours of nutritional study than general practitioners.

Diet and Nutrition: The French playwright Moliere said, "Eat to live, not live to eat." It's an excellent piece of advice. I aim for mindful, nutritious eating. Diet and nutrition are such complex subjects that I can't fully do justice to them here. Again, additional information and resources are posted on www.betsyhorn.com.

I believe that the best model for healthful eating is to emphasize food from plants. That would include fruits, vegetables, high-quality whole grains (no fast cooking oatmeal, please!) legumes and the right amounts of high quality oils, bean dishes, seeds, nuts, herbs and spices. I make a point of buying organic and/or local produce whenever possible and affordable. However, I do eat animal protein, finding it essential to my make-up. When I want a good detox, I do a liver/gallbladder cleanse and/or eat a macrobiotic diet for a week. I sometimes use the 5 Element Theory of balanced eating which is, essentially, a macrobiotic cuisine. After a few days of this cooking, I feel well-nourished, renewed and balanced. The sourcing of herbs and spices is important; again, more information on that issue is provided on my website. I tend to think of animal protein mostly as a condiment, an extra. When I eat it, I choose hand-sized portions. In general, I always want high fiber and good fats, plant chemicals and flavonoids. Making sure that I have diverse range and colors of vegetables on my daily menu is a good visual reminder, as is looking to see what is in season and eating local produce, if possible. (As I do not wish to appear a Pollyanna, I do go "off the wagon", especially in the summer when lobster is available and in Scotland where lean venison is on offer.)

Our lives can get so rushed, it's difficult to eat regularly, but I do so. I usually make a greens and fruit smoothie for breakfast, including nuts and seeds as well as a quinoa, amaranth and seaweed organic protein powder. (I recommend the Eveliza and Alen brands, which are available through my website.) Eating the evening meal on the early side allows for better digestion and sleep, allowing the digestive tract and inner organs more time to relax.

I use apple cider, balsamic or ubeboshi plum or rice vinegars in salad dressings, as my research suggests that they are the healthiest options, and I'm vigilant about getting enough Omega 3 essential fatty acids. Eating the standard American diet today will produce a higher ratio of Omega 6 and 9, not the correct balance for a heart-healthy diet. My beloved doctor, John Postley, mentioned a study recommending a combination of olive and canola for heart health and I have followed suit.

I try to avoid genetically modified foods (GMO) as we really don't know what their long term effects may be. "Eat real food," is my advice, and don't eat anything your grandmother wouldn't recognize! There are a lot of so-called "Frankenfoods" being produced. It takes persistence and dedication to stay clear of them, but the effort may really pay off.

I believe in eating and buying local and organic products whenever affordable and available. They are often more flavorful and they allow you to avoid most chemicals and other toxins. An established immune system may not be as affected cumulatively by foods which have been sprayed with a combination of herbicides, pesticides and other chemicals, but research suggests that a child's incomplete immune system will be. I advise everyone to stay away from processed food as much as possible; it is usually full of high fructose corn syrup and other forms of sugar. Processed sugars are always unhealthful, especially when eaten in quantity.

I believe in staying away from dairy foods except for the occasional goat and sheep milk yoghurt or cheese. Unless you know the cow personally, most commercial dairies are combining the milk of hundreds, if not thousands, of animals, all with their own immune system issues. We have no idea what shots or medicines any one animal has received, not to mention antibiotic dosage. Singers stay away from dairy as it is thought to be mucus forming.

Dental Care: The mouth is full of microorganisms which, untended, can cause periodontal disease. Mainstream dentists say, "See your dentist or see your cardiologist." Some dentists go further: If your mouth is unhealthy, they believe the body as a whole is unhealthy. As readers of this book know, Dr. Rau and the Paracelsus Clinic agree, advocating the removal of amalgam (mercury) fillings and old root canals to clean up sources of infection.

I brush religiously using a toothpaste crafted from wild herbs called PerioPaste, available in my wellness store from Dr. Light. In addition, I make regular use of a WaterPik machine with an oral cleanser and a Rotobrush, also available from Dr. Light. As discussed in the book, I have had problematic teeth removed, replacing them with titanium implants and zirconium crowns as the latter may be less toxic than porcelain ones. The process has not always been pretty, either literally or figuratively, but I'm confident that it has improved my health and well-being overall.

Emotions and Homeostataic Balance: As my story makes clear, emotions are very much a part of physical health; the mind, body, and spirit are as one, inter-connected, and can't be separated. Keep your heart open; work on forgiveness, awareness and inhabiting the present moment (meditation helps.) If we are always thinking about what we will do tomorrow or what didn't get done yesterday, we are not present, just distracted. Avoid perfectionism. Let your uniqueness and radiance shine.

Common sense, moderation, discipline, self-awareness, and intelligent approaches to complex issues: I strive for all of these. And a bit of luck doesn't hurt, either!

Find a focus for your energy and do what you love—it often turns out to be the very best choice for your well-being, not just financial, but also physical and emotional. Keep learning and engaging. I have gone back to school and am continuing with Mind-Body certifications, learning short meditations and breathing exercises for use in my workshops. I stay mentally engaged through reading, studying, researching and writing. All of these activities keep me energized and looking toward the future.

Eurythmy: Created by Rudolf Steiner, Therapeutic Eurythmy was introduced to me by Michael Falkner at the Paracelsus Clinic; I later explored it further with Seth Morrison, a practitioner in New York State. It combines exercises that require movement and responses to certain letters of the alphabet. I have found them profoundly useful in calming my inner spirit and self, also reducing body tension. A sequence takes no more than ten minutes, so Eurythmy can be practiced even when time is short. I practice often but especially when I am over-stressed. Eurythmy serves many purposes, addressing body, mind, soul and spirit. It is too complex to describe easily but I hope to do a short video for my site, when time permits.

Health and Wellness Support Team: My book tells the story of my search for and work with practitioners in a variety of fields and specialties. The comfort I feel with them is crucial to the activities we do together; I have deep trust in each. Find and consult with a practitioner you both like and trust, and of course, make sure you receive regular full checkups.

In addition to trusting my "team," I also respect my own instincts, which sometimes prompt me to ask questions or make choices that are not precisely what is recommended to me. As women, we must educate ourselves about our bodies, know both their strengths and weaknesses, and learn to listen for what they need. Our health is best when we are fully active participants in maintaining it: open to expert advice, but not overly deferential or submissive to plans that don't feel right.

Hormones: I have taken bio-identical hormones since my cancer and feel that they have contributed in many ways to my well-being. We have estrogen receptors all through the body. Studies show that estrogen, for example, enhances learning and memory and improves fine motor skills. It also affects mood, regulates body temperature and sleep, and helps avoid the thinning of vaginal tissues as well as loss of libido. It may also help with bone health. Progesterone has sedative effects and helps regulate both sleep and anxiety. In contrast, I believe that synthetic hormone replacement can be harmful.

This is a choice that each menopausal woman must make for herself, but luckily today there are both more healthy options, and more sound information (some of which is offered on my website), than ever before.

Kegel Exercises: To perform a short series, twice a day while in bed, has helped me enormously. As we age, the sphincter and urinary muscles may relax not only due to aging, but perhaps as a result of nerve damage because of chemo. A series will be available on the website at some future date. Stay tuned, please!

Life Balance: Don't spend all day at the computer. Get outside each day. If I am in a city, I make a point of walking through the park. Even when I am busiest, I try to make the time to get up, stretch, look out a window, and nurture my soul.

I believe that the arts play a healing and nurturing role in our lives. Readers of this book know that I'm a passionate music lover. I try to enjoy some music every day, and to savor all kinds of beauty from the natural to the man (and woman!)-made.

Massage: Long a staple of European health care, massage is both more widely available and affordable in the United States than ever, and offered in many different types and forms. I consider it a must, especially if I have been at the computer for hours on end. Among the multiple benefits of massage are relaxation, reduction of toxins and tensions throughout the body, and hydration of the tissues. Additionally, of course, it can help us feel pampered and cared for, an important component of well-being for women, given how often we find ourselves focused mainly on caring for others. There are too many different kinds of massage to mention here, but I love deep tissue, and general detox massages as well as foot reflexology and lymph drainage. Equally, there are many forms and varieties of self-massage and stretches we can learn to do for ourselves without spending money.

Meditation: I meditate twice a day, first thing in the morning and before bed in the evening. I am now trained in Advanced Mind Body Skills from the Center for Mind Body Medicine in Washington, D.C. and plan to acquire the second certification by 2014. I use many different kinds of meditations including Transcendental Meditation, which is customarily a 20-minute practice. There are shorter breathing or prayer meditations such as "Soft Belly" from the Center in Washington as well as hundreds of others. However, a yoga practice is meditative as well as is sitting and looking at the leaves fall, so we should all explore and find what works the best for each one of us. Meditation has been proven to quiet the mind and the heart.

Movement and Exercise: "Rhythm is the carrier of life," said Rudolf Steiner. Movement isn't just great for the body, it's beneficial to the emotions and spirit. Buy into your body and your dynamism. Walk, dance, run—simply, just move!

I love exercise, and I know that it helps keep me fit and pain free. Where I am dictates what I do: in the USA, I have free weights, bands, a hanging bar, and exercise balls of various sizes. In Scotland, I have Tiggy, our Border terrier, and friends to hike with. In Florida, I work out with Amy Svensson, who has me working on cardio, strength training, balance, bone health and stretching. She has devised and printed out workouts for me when I am on the road. When we work together, we do a good warm-up, cardiovascular and core strengthening as well as working all the muscle groups. I swim for endurance, enjoy ballroom dancing, am getting back into tennis, and take Pilates classes as well. I find that walking is one of the best, most relaxing ways to exercise, and something that is part of every day.

Even if you don't love exercise in general, there are so many forms of movement that it's always possible to find one you really enjoy. From kickboxing to Qigong to rock-wall-climbing, experiment a little and find one that truly suits you. Ballroom dancing is also a great workout!

Sauna: Far-infrared saunas come in several different sizes and represent one of the finest opportunities to detoxify heavy metals, boost the immune system, and improve many chronic conditions. For all of those reasons, it's my personal opinion that they may be beneficial for cancer patients as well as others. I use the High Tech Health Sauna, as I think it is the finest quality sauna on the market (found in the wellness store). These saunas can be assembled in less than an hour, including unpacking, as they are beautifully constructed and simply clip together.

Sleep: Good sleep is essential for cellular repair. Sleep, good and bad, goes through phases. On a cruise recently, I slept like a baby, but sometimes I'm not so lucky.

Wine or other alcohol with dinner is great, but in excess it can contribute to the "4 a.m. wake-ups" because alcohol suppresses the important and restorative REM cycle of sleep.

There are many herbal remedies which are useful for sleep. I particularly like the homeopathic drops from Ceres, a Swiss manufacturer, available through many homeopathic practitioners in the USA. Their Passiflora (passion flower) and Valeriana (valerian) drops are excellent. Low-dose melatonin also works well. Melatonin is a hormone, so it is wise to be careful and source it well. Apparently, one half to one milligram is a no-problem dose. I very occasionally use a generic Xanax tablet when I am having problems. If I wake up, for whatever reason, and am in the middle of a dream, I try to stay in it, as I've learned that there is a 50% chance the brain will take me back to a sleep state on its own. We all have different sensitivities to light and to food. I am finding that an eye mask enables me to sleep longer in the morning and that eating a light supper fairly early with a long period after to digest helps as well. The liver will have done most of its work if we eat light and don't go to bed right away.

Stress: Some stress is unavoidable, and certain kinds can be helpful in the short term to show us what's not working in our lives. But on-going, long-term stress can cause illnesses of all kinds.

As women, we often underplay stress in our willingness to help others and our need to appear to be coping. Held-in anger, repressed feelings, depression and anxiety contribute to stress and strain on the cells and organs. Wherever possible, our goal should be to acknowledge suppressed feelings, resolve psychological conflicts, and clean up unfinished emotional business. This is often easier said than done, as my own story shows, but even gradual progress in this direction makes a difference. Talking or writing out to express negative or angry emotions can help bring up and out some of the real reasons behind these feelings.

I believe that it's especially important to address anger so that you can leave it behind. Unacknowledged, it is a corrupting force both for the insides and relationships. Work as hard as you can on forgiveness. Get it out, whatever is bothering you. Wherever an issue is "stuck," whether in work, a relationship, or family of origin, it helps to express and to talk, especially to a professional counselor, often clarifying the real reason for the anger and leading us to more self-knowledge and personal growth.

Supplements: Food is always our best supplement. However, research demonstrates that non-organic food may be missing phytonutrients still present in organic, local produce. If you can't buy the latter, supplementation may be the only answer. Remember that vitamins are not only feeding you but other critters, as we have billions of micro-organisms within our bodies who are also needing nourishment. Choose carefully and preferably with the assistance of a qualified dietitian, nutritionist or naturopath—someone you have researched and can trust. Blood work can tell you what nutrients are missing—for example, Vitamin D, which is essential but often lacking in women. I have chosen only one or two anti-oxidants. I take both CoQ10 and curcumin, which is derived from turmeric, also known as the great cell cleaner. Among my supplements are Vitamin D, a strong, food based multi-vitamin, 1000 mil. Vitamin C, a general vitamin B complex , a fish oil capsule, a pro-biotic and selenium drops, all taken daily. Others may slip in to the mix from time to time, but that's the general format.

Water: Most of us are chronically dehydrated, a problem that increases as we age. When we make sure we're well hydrated, our energy comes back and we enjoy a feeling of renewal.

I begin the day with two glasses of warm water first thing in the morning; it's a wonderful way to lubricate the body and flush out toxins. You can use vegetable water if you are inclined, or add some fresh lemon juice to add alkalinity to the mixture. To keep myself well-hydrated when I'm out and around without problematic plastic water bottles, I have purchased a glass thermos, to be filled daily and taken with me, sometimes adding a tablespoon of cider vinegar for alkalinity. I'd like to reduce the mountain of plastic empties which we are producing daily and throwing away.

As the body can't absorb great amounts of water at one time, I don't gulp; instead, I try to drink steadily throughout the day. Mealtime is an exception: drinking water with the meal is thought to dissolve the digestive enzymes we need to break down our food. I avoid ice and extremely cold drinks at all times, as I don't believe they are good for the internal organs. Carbonated water is also unhealthy. If I become bored with drinking plain water, I might add some unsweetened organic apple or cranberry juice. I often drink light herbal teas, which are good sources of hydration if you drink them without sugar or other additives.

The integrity of the global water supply, including that of the United States, becomes more and more problematic and compromised over time. Hormones, antibiotics, pesticides, coliform bacteria and a myriad of other toxins have entered the water supply in many, if not all parts of the world, including the USA. Older water treatment facilities are not always geared to remove 21st century contaminants, such as mercury. Water in bottles is another problem; it's impossible to determine how far the water has travelled or the nature of the source, the plastic used in the bottling may be unhealthy, and of course they are wasteful and damaging to the environment.

I purify my water at home with an AKAI ionizing water machine which also disinfects with ultraviolet light and uses electrolysis to concentrate the minerals already existing in your tap water. (It's made in Japan, but available in the States through High Tech Health.) It can filter out many of the chemicals and particulate matter in tap water, as its micro-filter is very fine. It also brings the water to a high pH by separating out the acidic water, the acidulated water by-product being excellent both for our skin and our plants. Alkaline-ion water is an excellent anti-oxidant, helpful in reducing internal 'rust' or the free radicals which break down our health over time.

Yoga: Yoga can help us find and address our physical strengths and weaknesses. It works the kidneys and the adrenal glands as well as other organs, helping to create homeostasis in the system. Certain yoga postures or asanas balance neurotransmitters such as serotonin, providing a sense of well-being. (Twists and backbends are especially helpful for stimulating serotonin, as there are twelve serotonin receptor sites in the intestines.) "We have an outward and internal rhythm or harmony, like a well-balanced orchestra," Karin Stephan, my Massachusetts yoga teacher, says. In addition, it has an emotional and spiritual component. Yoga can help maintain harmony, keeping body, mind and spirit in balance.

I have a daily practice in Iyengar yoga, which I chose for its basis in good alignment. My routine includes headstand and shoulder stands—poses that work the thymus, pituitary, and thyroid glands. I find that even ten minutes is centering, calming to the mind and great for the organs. As described in the book, I always think of calming my sympathetic nervous system, to get me out and away from 'the flight or fight response." Unfortunately, many, if not most of us, live in that mode due to the constant stream of over-stimulation and "noise" our society delivers.

There are many schools and forms of yoga, so each woman can choose the kind that feels best to her. Experiment a bit, take a few different classes. Be aware of symptoms and know—and trust—what your body tells you.

Writing and sharing this toolbox with you has been a pleasure. If it offers new information or reinforces your own thoughts, I'll be pleased. I remain "passionate about your health" and know that even small changes can lead to big improvements.

Resources

The practitioners discussed in this book, the products mentioned in the Toolbox, and a wealth of other resources can be found on my website at www.betsyhorn.com. I hope you'll visit me there for some further exploration.

About the Author

BETSY HORN hails from Connecticut and was educated there as well as in Switzerland and New York. She lived in New York City for many years, working in public relations, at Harper's Bazaar magazine and in the painting department at Sotheby's art auction house. Moving to London in the late 1960s, she raised two daughters while working as a freelance photographer and location finder for such magazines as British Vogue and Town & Country. Returning to New York, she studied acting with Robert Lewis, cofounder of The Actor's Studio, and Stella Adler; those experiences forging a later-in-life career as a cabaret singer. Diagnosed with ovarian cancer over a decade ago, she decided that if she beat it, she would devote part of the rest of her life to learning about the components of true wellness and then share her knowledge with others. As a motivational speaker, senior advocate, and creator of workshops and talks dedicated to dynamic aging, prevention of recurrence, and the power of change, she understands the remarkable possibilities for transformation that reside in life's challenges. Having experience with Advanced Mind Body skills from the Center for Mind-Body Medicine in Washington, D.C., she uses those techniques of stress reduction and short meditations in her work. She is working on a series of shorter books, The Common Sense Health Books, the first of which will be on the importance of oral health. At present holding the title "Ms. Senior Florida 2013," she is working to leave a legacy of better nutrition for seniors. She and her husband live in Florida as well as in an ancient castle in Scotland, which they share with their dog, Tiggy, and a friendly ghost.

AUG 0 1 2015

CPSIA information can be obtained at www.ICGtesting.com
Printed in the USA
LVOW07s1734140415

434548LV00002B/405/P